Copyright © 2023 par Cyrielle Dufresne

This book is a work of fiction. Names, characters, places, and incidents are the product of the author's imagination or are used fictitiously. Any resemblance to actual persons, living or dead, businesses, companies, events, or locales is entirely coincidental.

ISBN : 9798389982154
First edition, 2023

#1 «In a world of peace and love, music would be the universal language.» - Henry David Thoreau

#2 «Love does not rule; but it trains, and that is more.» - Johann Wolfgang von Goethe

#3 «Love is the expression of the one who loves, not of the one who is loved. Those who think they can love only the people they prefer do not love at all. Love discovers truths about individuals that others cannot see» - Soren Kierkegaard

#4 «Man must evolve for all human conflict a method which rejects revenge, aggression and retaliation. The foundation of such a method is love.» - Martin Luther King, Jr.

#5 «I am inclined to think that nothing could matter more than what people love. At any rate, I can think of no value that I would place higher. I would not want to live in a world without love.» - Daniel Dennett

#6 «Selflessness is like waiting in a hospital
In a badly-fitting suit on a cold wet morning.
Selfishness is like listening to good jazz
With drinks for further orders and a huge fire.» - Philip Larkin"

#7 «Find me now. Before someone else does.» - Haruki Murakami

#8 «Love endures when the lovers love many things together And not merely each other.» - Walter Lippmann

#9 «Love is the expression of one's values, the greatest reward you can earn for the moral qualities you have achieved in your character and person, the emotional price paid by one man for the joy he receives from the virtues of another.» - Ayn Rand

#10 «Discipline is a symbol of caring to a child.He needs guidance.If there is love, there is no such thing as being too tough with a child. A parent must also not be afraid to hang himself. If you have never been hated by your child, you have never been a parent.» - Bette Davis

#11 «Love is the whole and more than all.» - e. e. cummings

#12 «My heart is, and always will be, yours.» - Jane Austen

#13 «Getting divorced just because you don't love a man is almost as silly as getting married just because you do.» - Zsa Zsa Gabor

#14 «In women everything is heart, even the head.» - Jean Paul

#15 «If I know what love is, it is because of you.» - Hermann Hesse

#16 «True love in this differs from gold and clay, that to divide is not to take away. Love is like understanding, that grows bright, gazing on many truths.» - Percy Bysshe Shelley

#17 «I love you for the part of me that you bring out.» - Elizabeth Barrett Browning

#18 «We fell in love despite our differences, and once we did, something rare and beautiful was created.» - Nicholas Sparks

#19 «When the power of love overcomes the love of power the world will know peace.» - Jimi Hendrix

#20 «Science without religion is lame, religion without science is blind.» - Albert Einstein

#21 «Making love with a woman and sleeping with a woman are two separate passions, not merely different but opposite. Love does not make itself felt in the desire for copulation (a desire that extends to an infinite number of women) but in the desire for shared sleep (a desire limited to one woman).» - Milan Kundera

#22 «Love is an endless mystery, for it has nothing else to explain it.» - Rabindranath Tagore

#23 «Only the really plain people know about love - the very fascinating ones try so hard to create an impression that they soon exhaust their talents.» - Katharine Hepburn

#24 «Love gives itself; it is not bought.» - Henry Wadsworth Longfellow

#25 «Infinite love is the only truth. Everything else is illusion.» - David Icke

#26 «Definition of Love: A score of zero in tennis. I love thee with the breath, Smiles, tears of all my life.» - Elizabeth Barrett Browning

#27 «When we honestly ask ourselves which person in our lives means the most to us, we often find that it is those who, instead of giving much advice, solutions, or cures, have chosen rather to share our pain and touch our wounds with a gentle and tender hand.» - Henri Nouwen

#28 «The unconquerable pang of despised love.» - William Wordsworth

#29 «For mightier far

Than strength of nerve or sinew, or the sway
Of magic potent over sun and star,

Is love, though oft to agony distrest,
And though his favourite be feeble woman's breast.» - William Wordsworth"

#30 «Love is not a because, it's a no matter what.» - Jodi Picoult

#31 «The best romance is inside marriage; the finest love stories come after the wedding, not before.» - Irving Stone

#32 «A mighty pain to love it is,

And 'tis a pain that pain to miss;
But, of all pains, the greatest pain

Is to love, but love in vain.» - Abraham Cowley"

#33 «As long as one can admire and love, then one is young forever.» - Pablo Casals

#34 «Material progress and a higher standard of living bring us greater comfort and health, but do not lead to a transformation of the mind, which is the only thing capable of providing lasting peace. Profound happiness, unlike fleeting pleasures, is spiritual in nature. It depends on the happiness of others and it is based on love and affection.» - Dalai Lama

#35 «You can give without loving, but you can never love without giving.» - Robert Louis Stevenson

#36 «Love is the voice under all silences, the hope which has no opposite in fear. . .» - e. e. cummings

#37 «When we feel love and kindness toward others, it not only makes others feel loved and cared for, but it helps us also to develop inner happiness and peace.» - Dalai Lama

#38 «When you have seen as much of life as I have, you will not underestimate the power of obsessive love.» - J. K. Rowling

#39 «Let your love flow out on all living things.» - William Styron

#40 «We let it in, we give it out, and in the end what's it all about? It must be love.» - Kate Bush

#41 «The heart is not so constituted, and the only way to dispossess it of an old affection is by the expulsive power of a new one» - Thomas Chalmers

#42 «Love is, above all, the gift of oneself.» - Jean Anouilh

#43 «Where we love is home - home that our feet may leave, but not our hearts.» - Oliver Wendell Holmes Sr.

#44 «Love is the silent saying and saying of a single name.» - Mignon McLaughlin

#45 «I'm not saying that love always takes you to heaven. Your life can become a nightmare. But that said, it is worth taking the risk.» - Paulo Coelho

#46 «Some say we are responsible for those we love. Others know we are responsible for those who love us.» - Nikki Giovanni

#47 «He who wants to do good knocks at the gate: he who loves finds the door open.» - Rabindranath Tagore

#48 «Life without love is like a tree without blossoms or fruit.» - Khalil Gibran

#49 «Love grows by service.» - Charlotte Perkins Gilman

#50 «Let love flow so that it cleanses the world. Then man can live in peace, instead of the state of turmoil he has created through his past ways of life, with all those material interests and earthly ambitions.» - Sai Baba

#51 «Don't worry about losing. If it is right, it happens - The main thing is not to hurry. Nothing good gets away.» - John Steinbeck

#52 «It is with true love as it is with ghosts; everyone talks about it, but few have seen it.» - Francois de La Rochefoucauld

#53 «It is the passion that is in a kiss that gives to it its sweetness; it is the affection in a kiss that sanctifies it.» - Christian Nestell Bovee

#54 «We fell in love, despite our differences, and once we did, something rare and beautiful was created. For me, love like that has only happened once, and that's why every minute we spent together has been seared in my memory. I'll never forget a single moment of it.» - Nicholas Sparks

#55 «Beloved, let us love one another: for love is of God» - John the Apostle

#56 «Love is a perky elf dancing a merry little jig and then suddenly he turns on you with a miniature machine gun.» - Matt Groening

#57 «Each time you happen to me all over again.» - Edith Wharton

#58 «Every atom of your flesh is as dear to me as my own: in pain and sickness it would still be dear.» - Charlotte Bronte

#59 «The Gospel does not require anything good that man must furnish: not a good heart, not a good disposition, no improvement of his condition, no godliness, no love either of God or men........ It plants love into his heart and makes him capable of all good works. It demands nothing, but it gives all. Should not this fact make us leap for JOY?» - C. F. W. Walther

#60 «I love you because all the loves in the world are like different rivers flowing into the same lake where they meet and are transformed into a single love that becomes rain and blesses the earth.» - Paulo Coelho

#61 «For one pain endured with joy, we shall love the good God more forever.» - Therese of Lisieux

#62 «As love without esteem is capricious and volatile; esteem without love is languid and cold.» - Jonathan Swift

#63 «For our personal advancement in virtue and truth one quality is sufficient, namely, love; to advance humanity there must be two, love and intelligence; to accomplish the Great Work there must be three love, intelligence, and activity. And yet love is ever the root and the source.» - Louis Claude de Saint-Martin

#64 «There's always one who loves and one who lets himself be loved.» - W. Somerset Maugham

#65 «A woman has got to love a bad man once or twice in her life, to be thankful for a good one.» - Marjorie Kinnan Rawlings

#66 «Not one word, not one gesture of yours shall I, could I, ever forget.» - Leo Tolstoy

#67 «Don't marry a man to reform him - that's what reform schools are for.» - Mae West

#68 «I like not only to be loved, but also to be told I am loved.» - George Eliot

#69 «The truth is that there is only one terminal dignity - love. And the story of a love is not important - what is important is that one is capable of love. It is perhaps the only glimpse we are permitted of eternity.» - Helen Hayes

#70 «Security is when I'm very much in love with somebody extraordinary who loves me back.» - Shelley Winters

#71 «Love, love, love – all the wretched cant of it, masking egotism, lust, masochism, fantasy under a mythology of sentimental postures, a welter of self-induced miseries and joys, blinding and masking the essential personalities in the frozen gestures of courtship, in the kissing and the dating and the desire, the compliments and the quarrels which vivify its barrenness.» - Germaine Greer

#72 «A man reserves his true and deepest love not for the species of woman in whose company he finds himself electrified and enkindled, but for that one in whose company he may feel tenderly drowsy.» - George Jean Nathan

#73 «Love isn't something you find. Love is something that finds you.» - Loretta Young

#74 «Faith makes all things possible... love makes all things easy.» - Dwight L. Moody

#75 «The afternoon knows what the morning never suspected.» - Robert Frost

#76 «I'm not sure this is a world I belong in anymore. I'm not sure that I want to wake up.» - Gayle Forman

#77 «I think we dream so we don't have to be apart so long. If we're in each other's dreams, we can play together all night.» - Bill Watterson

#78 «Therefore the best fortress is to be found in the love of the people, for although you may have fortresses they will not save you if you are hated by the people.» - Niccolo Machiavelli

#79 «A person starts to live when he can live outside himself.» - Albert Einstein

#80 «Watch out for intellect, because it knows so much it knows nothing and leaves you hanging upside down, mouthing knowledge as your heart falls out of your mouth.» - Anne Sexton

#81 «Take away love and our earth is a tomb.» - Robert Browning

#82 «Every lover is a soldier. (Love is a warfare.) [Lat., Militat omnis amans.]» - Ovid"

#83 «I'm aware of the mystery around us, so I write about coincidences, premonitions, emotions, dreams, the power of nature, magic.» - Isabel Allende

#84 «There is a place you can touch a woman that will drive her crazy. Her heart.» - Melanie Griffith

#85 «Speak low, if you speak love.» - William Shakespeare

#86 «Love is an abstract noun, something nebulous. And yet love turns out to be the only part of us that is solid, as the world turns upside down and the screen goes black.» - Martin Amis

#87 «You know what I am going to say. I love you. What other men may mean when they use that expression, I cannot tell. What I mean is that I am under the influence of some tremendous attraction which I have resisted in vain, and which overmasters me. You could draw me to fire, you could draw me to water, you could draw me to the gallows, you could draw me to any death, you could draw me to anything I have most avoided, you could draw me to any exposure and disgrace. This and the confusion of my thoughts, so that I am fit for nothing, is what I mean by your being the ruin of me.» - Charles Dickens

#88 «Love is not a business. It's not a transaction. It's not an exchange or something you get for doing something it's not a trade. It's a gift!» - Tony Robbins

#89 «The unhappy person resents it when you try to cheer him up, because that means he has to stop dwelling on himself and start paying attention to the universe. Unhappiness is the ultimate form of self-indulgence. When you're unhappy, you get to pay a lot of attention to yourself. You get to take yourself oh so very seriously.» - Tom Robbins

#90 «It is better to be loved by one person who knows your soul than millions who don't even know your phone number.» - Richard Paul Evans

#91 «For those who love... time is eternity.» - Henry Van Dyke

#92 «Nobody will ever love you quite the way you want them to. You just have to let them do their best.» - Axel

#93 «If everybody loves you, something is wrong. Find at least one enemy to keep you alert.» - Paulo Coelho

#94 «I have been astonished that men could die martyrs for their religion-- I have shuddered at it, I shudder no more. I could be martyred for my religion. Love is my religion and I could die for that. I could die for you. My Creed is Love and you are its only tenet.» - John Keats

#95 «Love is a promise, love is a souvenir, once given never forgotten, never let it disappear.» - John Lennon

#96 «I love you like a fat kid loves cake!» - Scott Adams

#97 «It is wrong to think that love comes from long companionship and persevering courtship. Love is the offspring of spiritual affinity and unless that affinity is created in a moment, it will not be created for years or even generations.» - Khalil Gibran

#98 «This was love: a string of coincidences that gathered significance and became miracles.» - Chimamanda Ngozi Adichie

#99 «I have a very strong feeling that the opposite of love is not hate - it's apathy. It's not giving a damn.» - Leo Buscaglia

#100 «Those who have never known the deep intimacy and the intense companionship of happy mutual love have missed the best thing that life has to give.» - Bertrand Russell

#101 «None of us has the power to make someone else love us. But we all have the power to give away love, to love other people. And if we do so, we change the kind of world we live in.» - Harold S. Kushner

#102 «We were two and had but one heart between us.» - Francois Villon

#103 «The garden of love is green without limit and yields many fruits other than sorrow or joy. Love is beyond either condition: without spring, without autumn, it is always fresh.» - Rumi

#104 «Not where I breathe, but where I love, I live.» - Robert Southwell

#105 «Never pretend to a love which you do not actually feel, for love is not ours to command.» - Alan Watts

#106 «A loving heart is the beginning of all knowledge.» - Thomas Carlyle

#107 «If my love were an ocean, there would be no more land. If my love were a desert, you would see only sand. If my love were a star- late at night, only light. And if my love could grow wings, I'd be soaring in flight.» - Jay Asher

#108 «We are shaped and fashioned by what we love.-

Henry Ward Beecher -
I never knew how to worship until I knew how to love.» - Johann Wolfgang von Goethe"

#109 «I fell in love with her when we were together, then fell deeper in love with her in the years we were apart.» - Nicholas Sparks

#110 «For above all, love is a sharing. Love is a power. Love is a change that takes place in our own heart. Sometimes it may change others, but always it changes us.» - James Dillet Freeman

#111 «The middle of the road is where the white line is - and that's the worst place to drive.» - Robert Frost

#112 «A moment of anger can destroy a lifetime of work, whereas a moment of love can break barriers that took a lifetime to build.» - Leon Brown

#113 «An archaeologist is the best husband a woman can have. The older she gets the more interested he is in her.» - Agatha Christie

#114 «There is always something left to love. And if you haven't learned that, you ain't learned nothing.» - Lorraine Hansberry

#115 «In my deepest wound I saw your glory, and it dazzled me.» - Saint Augustine

#116 «It takes courage to love, but pain through love is the purifying fire which those who love generously know. We all know people who are so much afraid of pain that they shut themselves up like clams in a shell and, giving out nothing, receive nothing and therefore shrink until life is a mere living death.» - Eleanor Roosevelt

#117 «The most precious possession that ever comes to a man in this world is a woman's heart.» - J. G. Holland

#118 «It's not what you do, but how much love you put into it that matters.» - Rick Warren

#119 «The simple lack of her is more to me than others' presence.» - Edward Thomas

#120 «No love, no friendship, can cross the path of our destiny without leaving some mark on it forever.» - Francois Mauriac

#121 «Love is that micro-moment of warmth and connection that you share with another living being» - Barbara Fredrickson

#122 «It is not that love is blind. It is that love sees with a painter's eye, finding the essence that renders all else background.» - Robert Breault

#123 «We can talk frankly about our defects only to those who recognise our qualities.» - Andre Maurois

#124 «Well-ordered self-love is right and natural.» - Thomas Aquinas

#125 «My dear, Find what you love and let it kill you. Let it drain you of your all. Let it cling onto your back and weigh you down into eventual nothingness. Let it kill you and let it devour your remains. For all things will kill you, both slowly and fastly, but it's much better to be killed by a lover. ~ Falsely yours» - Charles Bukowski

#126 «Once a man has won a woman's love, the love is his forever. He can only lose the woman.» - Robert Breault

#127 «Young love is a flame; very pretty, often very hot and fierce, but still only light and flickering. The love of the older and disciplined heart is as coals, deep-burning, unquenchable.» - Henry Ward Beecher

#128 «A loving heart is the truest wisdom.» - Charles Dickens

#129 «It may be true that the law cannot make a man love me, but it can keep him from lynching me, and I think that's pretty important.» - Martin Luther King, Jr.

#130 «If I could be anything in the world I would want to be a teardrop because I would be born in your eyes, live on your cheeks, and die on your lips.» - Mary, Queen of Scots

#131 «What's love got to do with it?» - Tina Turner

#132 «Love is the law of life.» - Mahatma Gandhi

#133 «Love built on beauty, soon as beauty, dies.» - John Donne

#134 «In art as in love, instinct is enough.» - Anatole France

#135 «Love is like the wind, you can't see it but you can feel it.» - Nicholas Sparks

#136 «Love is God, and to die means that I, a particle of love, shall return to the general and eternal source.» - Leo Tolstoy

#137 «The greatest weakness of most humans is their hesitancy to tell others how much they love them while they're alive.» - Orlando Aloysius Battista

#138 «Art and love are the same thing: It's the process of seeing yourself in things that are not you.» - Chuck Klosterman

#139 «Romance is the glamour which turns the dust of everyday life into a golden haze.» - Elinor Glyn

#140 «Giving and receiving love is vital to human existence. It is the glue that binds couples, families, communities, cultures, and nations.» - G. Frank Lawlis

#141 «A lover without indiscretion is no lover at all.» - Thomas Hardy

#142 «Those who are faithful know only the trivial side of love: it is the faithless who know love's tragedies.» - Oscar Wilde

#143 «Oh, life is a glorious cycle of song, a medley of extemporanea, And love is a thing that can never go wrong, and I am Marie of Romania.» - Dorothy Parker

#144 «I love Love -- though he has wings, And like light can flee.» - Percy Bysshe Shelley

#145 «It is certain that there is no other passion which does produce such contrary effects in so great a degree. But this may be said for love, that if you strike it out of the soul, life would be insipid, and our being but half animated.» - Joseph Addison

#146 «All a girl really wants is for one guy to prove to her that they are not all the same.» - Marilyn Monroe

#147 «In doing something, do it with love or never do it at all.» - Mahatma Gandhi

#148 «Love is the enchanted dawn of every heart.» - Alphonse de Lamartine

#149 «This is where it all begins. Everything starts here, today.» - David Nicholls

#150 «You are your only hope, because we're not changing until you do. Our job is to keep coming at you, as hard as we can, with everything that angers, upsets, or repulses you, until you understand. We love you that much, whether we're aware of it or not. The whole world is about you.» - Byron Katie

#151 «But to see her was to love her, Love but her, and love forever.» - Robert Burns

#152 «Love is the only thing that we can carry with us when we go, and it makes the end so easy.» - Louisa May Alcott

#153 «When it's over, I want to say: all my life I was a bride married to amazement. I was the bridegroom, taking the world into my arms.» - Mary Oliver

#154 «True love will triumph in the end—which may or may not be a lie, but if it is a lie, it's the most beautiful lie we have.» - John Green

#155 «The sweetest of all sounds is that of the voice of the woman we love.» - Jean de la Bruyere

#156 «I learned the real meaning of love. Love is absolute loyalty. People fade, looks fade, but loyalty never fades. You can depend so much on certain people, you can set your watch by them. And that's love, even if it doesn't seem very exciting.» - Sylvester Stallone

#157 «At the end of the day people won't remember what you said or did, they will remember how you made them feel.» - Maya Angelou

#158 «Love has no conditions. When we put conditions, when we put barriers and boundaries, then we lose love. Love is condition-less. Love is barrier-less. Look at the moon, sun, stars, trees. . . they are just on for everyone. When our love also flows for everyone, you become very natural.» - Chidanand Saraswati

#159 «Love is the offspring of spiritual affinity and unless that affinity is created in a moment, it will not be created for years or even generations.» - Nikki Giovanni

#160 «Hate the sin, love the sinner.» - Mahatma Gandhi

#161 «Love Is Stronger Than Pride» - Marquis de Sade

#162 «With love and patience, nothing is impossible.» - Daisaku Ikeda

#163 «I think we ought to live happily ever after.» - Diana Wynne Jones

#164 «Oh, rather give me commentators plain, Who with no deep researches vex the brain; Who from the dark and doubtful love to run, And hold their glimmering tapers to the sun.» - George Crabbe

#165 «Till it has loved, no man or woman can become itself.» - Emily Dickinson

#166 «Poets often describe love as an emotion that we can't control, one that overwhelms logic and common sense. That's what it was like for me. I didn't plan on falling in love with you, and I doubt if you planned on falling in love with me. But once we met, it was clear that neither of us could control what was happening to us. We fell in love, despite our differences, and once we did, something rare and beautiful was created. For me, love like that has happened only once, and that's why every minute we spent together has been seared in my memory. I'll never forget a single moment of it.» - Nicholas Sparks

#167 «LOVE, n. A temporary insanity curable by marriage or by removal of the patient from the influences under which he incurred the disorder.» - Ambrose Bierce

#168 «What's this?" he demanded, looking from Clary to his companions, as if they might know what she was doing there. "It's a girl," Jace said,recovering his composure. "Surely you've seen girls before, Alec. Your sister Isabelle is one.» - Cassandra Clare

#169 «Open your heart and take us in, Love-love and me.» - William Ernest Henley

#170 «Perhaps, after all, romance did not come into one's life with pomp and blare, like a gay knight riding down; perhaps it crept to one's side like an old friend through quiet ways; perhaps it revealed itself in seeming prose, until some sudden shaft of illumination flung athwart its pages betrayed the rhythm and the music, perhaps . . . perhaps . . . love unfolded naturally out of a beautiful friendship, as a golden-hearted rose slipping from its green sheath.» - Lucy Maud Montgomery

#171 «Love is an attempt to change a piece of a dream world into reality.» - Theodor Reik

#172 «I love you also means I love you more than anyone loves you, or has loved you, or will love you, and also, I love you in a way that no one loves you, or has loved you, or will love you, and also, I love you in a way that I love no one else, and never have loved anyone else, and never will love anyone else.» - Jonathan Safran Foer

#173 «Can miles truly separate you from friends... If you want to be with someone you love, aren't you already there?» - Richard Bach

#174 «The way to love anything is to realize that it may be lost.» - Gilbert K. Chesterton

#175 «Happiness and peace will come to earth only as the light of love and human compassion enter the souls of men.» - David O. McKay

#176 «I cannot think well of a man who sports with any woman's feelings; and there may often be a great deal more suffered than a stander-by can judge of.» - Jane Austen

#177 «As soon go kindle fire with snow, as seek to quench the fire of love with words.» - William Shakespeare

#178 «The sun will stand as your best man

And whistle
When you have found the courage

To marry forgiveness

When you have found the courage
to marry Love.» - Hafez"

#179 «Anyone who is in love is making love the whole
time, even when they're not. When two bodies meet, it is
just the cup overflowing. They can stay together for hours,
even days. They begin the dance one day and finish it the
next, or - such is the pleasure they experience - they may
never finish it. No eleven minutes for them.» - Paulo
Coelho

#180 «We are each of us angels with only one wing, and
we can only fly by embracing one another.» - Luciano De
Crescenzo

#181 «Love is the greatest touch-up artist of all.» - Robert
Breault

#182 «Love is life. All, everything that I understand, I
understand only because I love. Everything is, everything
exists, only because I love. Everything is united by it alone.
Love is God, and to die means that I, a particle of love,
shall return to the general and eternal source.» - Leo
Tolstoy

#183 «Life is pain and the enjoyment of love is an anesthetic.» - Cesare Pavese

#184 «A successful marriage requires falling in love many times, always with the same person.» - Mignon McLaughlin
#185 «Understand that you own nothing. Everything that surrounds you is temporary. Only the love in your heart will last forever.» - Leon Brown

#186 «Accustom yourself continually to make many acts of love, for they enkindle and melt the soul.» - Teresa of Avila

#187 «Live well laugh often and love much.» - Bessie Anderson Stanley

#188 «True love is eternal, infinite, and always like itself. It is equal and pure, without violent demonstrations: it is seen with white hairs and is always young in the heart.» - Honore de Balzac

#189 «Money can't buy me love.» - John Lennon

#190 «When you love a man, he becomes more than a body. His physical limbs expand, and his outline recedes, vanishes. He is rich and sweet and right. He is part of the world, the atmosphere, the blue sky and the blue water.» - Gwendolyn Brooks

#191 «If conversation was the lyrics, laughter was the music, making time spent together a melody that could be replayed over and over without getting stale.» - Nicholas Sparks

#192 «The scariest thing about distance is that you don't know whether they'll miss you or forget you.» - Nicholas Sparks

#193 «A man who loves you the most is the man who tells you the most truth about yourself.» - Robert Murray M'Cheyne

#194 «It is always possible to bind together a considerable number of people in love, so long as there are other people left over to receive the manifestations of their aggressiveness.» - Sigmund Freud

#195 «The best and most beautiful things in the world cannot be seen or even touched - they must be felt with the heart.» - Helen Keller

#196 «Madame, it is an old word and each one takes it new and wears it out himself. It is a word that fills with meaning as a bladder with air and the meaning goes out of it as quickly. It may be punctured as a bladder is punctured and patched and blown up again and if you have not had it does not exist for you. All people talk of it, but those who have had it are marked by it, and I would not wish to speak of it further since of all things it is the most ridiculous to talk of and only fools go through it many times.» - Ernest Hemingway

#197 «It's not the face, but the expressions on it. It's not the voice, but what you say. It's not how you look in that body, but the thing you do with it. You are beautiful.» - Stephenie Meyer

#198 «If I place love above everything, it is because for me it is the most desperate, the most despairing state of affairs imaginable.» - Andre Breton

#199 «Love is the only freedom in the world because it so elevates the spirit that the laws of humanity and the phenomena of nature do not alter its course.» - Khalil Gibran

#200 «Wherever you find real love, you will also find humility. Remember something: humility is not a weak and timid quality. Too often we feel that humility is a sign of weakness. This is not so. It is the sign of strength and security.» - Kathryn Kuhlman

#201 «All you need is love.» - John Lennon

#202 «If you can stay in love for more than two years, you're on something.» - Fran Lebowitz

#203 «It hurts to love wide open stretching the muscles... It hurts to thwart the reflexes of grab, of clutch; to love and let go again and again.» - Marge Piercy

#204 «And then I asked him with my eyes to ask again yes and then he asked me would I yes and his heart was going like mad and yes I said yes I will yes.» - James Joyce

#205 «When you're a teenager and you're in love, it's obvious to everyone but you and the person you're in love with.» - John Scalzi

#206 «We can give without loving, but we can't love without giving. In fact, love is nothing unless we give it to someone.» - John Wooden

#207 «In all the world, there is no heart for me like yours. In all the world, there is no love for you like mine.» - Maya Angelou

#208 «Here are fruits, flowers, leaves and branches, and here is my heart which beats only for you.» - Paul Verlaine

#209 «Don't speak to me about your religion; first show it to me in how you treat other people. Don't tell me how much you love your God; show me in how much you love all God's children. Don't preach to me your passion for your faith; teach me through your compassion for your neighbors. In the end, I'm not as interested in what you have to tell or sell as I am in how you choose to live and give.» - Cory Booker

#210 «Love is the river of life in this world.» - Henry Ward Beecher

#211 «In the arithmetic of love, one plus one equals everything, and two minus one equals nothing.» - Mignon McLaughlin

#212 «Today I begin to understand what love must be, if it exists... When we are parted, we each feel the lack of the other half of ourselves. We are incomplete like a book in two volumes of which the first has been lost. That is what I imagine love to be: incompleteness in absence.» - Edmond de Goncourt

#213 «I'd learned that some things are best kept secret.» - Nicholas Sparks

#214 «God loves the world through us.» - Mother Teresa

#215 «No cord or cable can draw so forcibly, or bind so fast, as love can do with a single thread.» - Robert Burton

#216 «We've got this gift of love, but love is like a precious plant. You can't just accept it and leave it in the cupboard or just think it's going to get on by itself. You've got to keep watering it. You've got to really look after it and nurture it.» - John Lennon

#217 «Perhaps the feelings that we experience when we are in love represent a normal state. Being in love shows a person who he should be.» - Anton Chekhov

#218 «When love is in excess, it brings a man no honor, no worthiness.» - Euripides

#219 «And you will remember that love is not getting, but giving; not a wild dream of pleasure, and a madness of desire — oh no, love is not that — it is goodness, and honour, and peace, and pure living — yes, love is that; and it is the best thing in the world, and the thing that lives longest.» - Henry Van Dyke

#220 «What's in a name? That which we call a rose by any other name would smell as sweet.» - William Shakespeare

#221 «The power of love is a curious thing, make one man weep, make another man sing. Change a hawk to a little white dove, more than a feeling, that's the power of love.» - Huey Lewis

#222 «This was love at first sight, love everlasting: a feeling unknown, unhoped for, unexpected--in so far as it could be a matter of conscious awareness; it took entire possession of him, and he understood, with joyous amazement, that this was for life.» - Thomas Mann

#223 «Love is not love
Which alters when it alteration finds,

Or bends with the remover to remove.
O, no! It is an ever-fixed mark,

That looks on tempests and is never shaken.
It is the star to every wandering bark,

Whose worth's unknown, although his height be taken.» - William Shakespeare"

#224 «If he loved with all the powers of his puny being, he couldn't love as much in eighty years as I could in a day.» - Emily Bronte

#225 «Only love makes fruitful the soul.» - John Galsworthy

#226 «One advantage of marriage is that, when you fall out of love with him or he falls out of love with you, it keeps you together until you fall in again.» - Judith Viorst

#227 «When you loved me I gave you the whole sun and stars to play with. I gave you eternity in a single moment, strength of the mountains in one clasp of your arms, and the volume of all the seas in one impulse of your soul.» - George Bernard Shaw

#228 «The greatest pleasure of life is love.» - Euripides

#229 «Let love flow so that it cleanses the world.» - Sathya Sai Baba

#230 «There is no scarcity of opportunity to make a living at what you love; there's only scarcity of resolve to make it happen.» - Wayne Dyer

#231 «When you love someone you let them take care of you.» - Jodi Picoult

#232 «I love you not only for what you are, but for what I am when I am with you» - Roy Croft

#233 «We've all got both light and dark inside us. What matters is the part we choose to act on. That's who we really are.» - J. K. Rowling

#234 «There are only really a few stories to tell in the end, and betrayal and the failure of love is one of those good stories to tell.» - Sean Lennon

#235 «I try to make sense of life. I try to keep myself open to people and to laughter and to love and to have faith.» - Thea Bowman

#236 «Love is not a product of reasonings and statistics. It just comes-none knows whence-and cannot explain itself.» - Mark Twain

#237 «Look after my heart - I've left it with you.» - Stephenie Meyer

#238 «I love being in love.» - Brittany Murphy

#239 «Loving people live in a loving world. Hostile people live in a hostile world. Same world.» - Wayne Dyer

#240 «The supreme happiness of life is the conviction that we are loved.» - Victor Hugo

#241 «In love the paradox occurs that two beings become one and yet remain two.» - Erich Fromm

#242 «Some day, the world will discover that, without thought, there can be no love.» - Ayn Rand

#243 «I learned that it is the weak who are cruel, and that gentleness is to be expected only from the strong.» - Leo Rosten

#244 «If you want a love message to be heard, it has got to be sent out. To keep a lamp burning, we have to keep putting oil in it.» - Mother Teresa

#245 «Among those whom I like or admire, I can find no common denominator, but among those whom I love, I can: all of them make me laugh.» - W. H. Auden

#246 «Love is an irresistible desire to be irresistibly desired.» - Robert Frost

#247 «Love is a special word, and I use it only when I mean it. You say the word too much and it becomes cheap.» - Ray Charles

#248 «Love is the poetry of the senses.» - Honore de Balzac

#249 «Love is a second life.» - Joseph Addison

#250 «Things are beautiful if you love them.» - Jean Anouilh

#251 «if you love two people at the same time, choose the second. Because if you really loved the first one, you wouldn't have fallen for the second.» - Johnny Depp

#252 «As you dissolve into love, your ego fades. You're not thinking about loving; you're just being love, radiating like the sun.» - Ram Dass

#253 «On the path to love, impossibilities are resolved by turning non-love into love.» - Deepak Chopra

#254 «To fear love is to fear life, and those who fear life are already three parts dead.» - Bertrand Russell

#255 «The beginning and the end of love are both marked by embarrassment when the two find themselves alone. [Fr., Le commencement et le declin de l'amour se font sentir par l'embarras ou l'on est de se trouver seuls.]» - Jean de la Bruyere"

#256 «It has been wisely said that we cannot really love anybody at whom we never laugh.» - Agnes Repplier

#257 «Forgiveness is the final form of love.» - Reinhold Niebuhr

#258 «Love is the cure, for your pain will keep giving birth to more pain until your eyes constantly exhale love as effortlessly as your body yields its scent.» - Rumi

#259 «Everybody can be great...because anybody can serve. You don't have to have a college degree to serve. You don't have to make your subject and verb agree to serve. You only need a heart full of grace. A soul generated by love.» - Martin Luther King, Jr.

#260 «One word

Frees us of all the weight and pain of life:
That word is love.» - Sophocles"

#261 «I guess, when you get down to it, a loving touch compensates for an unskilled hand about everywhere except in an airplane cockpit.» - Robert Breault

#262 «If our love is only a will to possess, it is not love.» - Nhat Hanh

#263 «Don't wake up a woman in love. Let her dream, so that she does not weep when she returns to her bitter reality» - Mark Twain

#264 «We're all a little weird. And life is a little weird. And when we find someone whose weirdness is compatible with ours, we join up with them and fall into mutually satisfying weirdness — and call it love — true love.» - Robert Fulghum

#265 «Love is but the discovery of ourselves in others, and the delight in the recognition.» - Alexander Smith

#266 «Love is our only reason for living and the only purpose of life. We live for the sake of love, and we live seeking love... it is not surprising that we keep looking for love. All of us are nothing but vibrations of love. We are sustained by love, and in the end we merge back into love.» - Swami Muktananda

#267 «Perhaps it's because it's incredible to meet someone and say: with this person, I'm happy.» - Anna Gavalda

#268 «Every woman deserves a man to ruin her lipstick, not her mascara» - Charlotte Tilbury

#269 «And when love speaks, the voice of all the gods makes Heaven drowsy with the harmony.» - William Shakespeare

#270 «I love you because I love you, because it would be impossible not to love you. I love you without question, without calculation, without reason good or bad, faithfully, with all my heart and soul, and every faculty.» - Juliette Drouet

#271 «Spread love everywhere you go. Let no one ever come to you without leaving happier.» - Mother Teresa

#272 «Don't be reckless with other peoples hearts. And don't put up with people that are reckless with yours.» - Kurt Vonnegut

#273 «Loving someone and having them love you back is the most precious thing in the world.» - Nicholas Sparks

#274 «Love is a symbol of eternity. It wipes out all sense of time, destroying all memory of a beginning and all fear of an end.» - Madame de Stael

#275 «We choose those we like; with those we love, we have no say in the matter.» - Mignon McLaughlin

#276 «I finally understood what true love meant...love meant that you care for another person's happiness more than your own, no matter how painful the choices you face might be.» - Nicholas Sparks

#277 «Nothing we do, however virtuous, can be accomplished alone; therefore we are saved by love.» - Reinhold Niebuhr

#278 «I hate being so emotionally slutty. I need to stop loving everyone I have a long conversation with.» - Sara Quin

#279 «The arms of love encompass you with your present, your past, your future, the arms of love gather you together.» - Antoine de Saint-Exupery

#280 «Self-love, my liege, is not so vile a sin, as self-neglecting.» - William Shakespeare

#281 «In order to be an immaculate member of a flock of sheep, one must above all be a sheep oneself.» - Albert Einstein

#282 «It is impossible to love and to be wise.» - Francis Bacon

#283 «Love is a smoke made with the fume of sighs.» - William Shakespeare

#284 «But love is always new. Regardless of whether we love once, twice, or a dozen times in our life, we always face a brand-new situation. Love can consign us to hell or to paradise, but it always takes us somewhere. We simply have to accept it, because it is what nourishes our existence. We have to take love where we find it, even if that means hours, days, weeks of disappointment and sadness.» - Paulo Coelho

#285 «Let this be my last word, that I trust in thy love.» - Rabindranath Tagore

#286 «Forget about enlightenment. Sit down wherever you are and listen to the wind that is singing in your veins. Feel the love, the longing and the fear in your bones. Open your heart to who you are, right now, not who you would like to be. Not the saint you're striving to become. But the being right here before you, inside you, around you. All of you is holy. You're already more and less than whatever you can know. Breathe out, look in, let go.» - John Welwood

#287 «Are we in love with God or just His stuff?» - Francis Chan

#288 «Hatred paralyzes life; love releases it. Hatred confuses life; love harmonizes it. Hatred darkens life; love illuminates it.» - Martin Luther King, Jr.

#289 «Whoso loves, believes in the impossible» - Elizabeth Barrett Browning

#290 «Love is the wisdom of the fool and the folly of the wise.» - Samuel Johnson

#291 «Your mother died to save you. If there is one thing Voldemort cannot understand, it is love. Love as powerful as your mother's for you leaves it's own mark. To have been loved so deeply, even though the person who loved us is gone, will give us some protection forever.» - J. K. Rowling

#292 «Let the first impulse pass, wait for the second.» - Baltasar Gracian

#293 «But love, I've come to understand, is more than three words mumbled before bedtime. Love is sustained by action, a pattern of devotion in the things we do for each other every day.» - Nicholas Sparks

#294 «Love has no age, no limit; and no death.» - John Galsworthy

#295 «Two persons love in one another the future good which they aid one another to unfold.» - Margaret Fuller

#296 «I am catastrophically in love with you.» - Cassandra Clare

#297 «Come out of the circle of time

And into the circle of love.» - Rumi"

#298 «The only reward for love is the experience of loving.» - John le Carre

#299 «Love and magic have a great deal in common. They enrich the soul, delight the heart. And they both take practice.» - Nora Roberts

#300 «I love being married. It's so great to find that one special person you want to annoy for the rest of your life.» - Rita Rudner

#301 «Hurt people hurt people. That's how pain patterns gets passed on, generation after generation after generation. Break the chain today. Meet anger with sympathy, contempt with compassion, cruelty with kindness. Greet grimaces with smiles. Forgive and forget about finding fault. Love is the weapon of the future.» - Yehuda Berg

#302 «Romance has been elegantly defined as the offspring of fiction and love.» - Benjamin Disraeli

#303 «This is a good sign, having a broken heart. It means we have tried for something.» - Elizabeth Gilbert

#304 «Love is fed by the imagination, by which we become wiser than we know, better than we feel, nobler than we are: by which we can see life as a whole, by which and by which alone we can understand others in their real and their ideal relation. Only what is fine, and finely conceived can feed love. But anything will feed hate.» - Oscar Wilde

#305 «And next time you're planning to injure yourself to get me attention, just remember that a little sweet talk works wonders.» - Cassandra Clare

#306 «We can't command our love, but we can our actions.» - Arthur Conan Doyle

#307 «A friendship that like love is warm; A love like friendship, steady.» - Thomas Moore

#308 «Bitterness imprisons life; love releases it. Bitterness paralyzes life; love empowers it. Bitterness sours life; love sweetens it. Bitterness sickens life; love heals it. Bitterness blinds life; love anoints its eyes.» - Harry Emerson Fosdick

#309 «If love is the soul of Christian existence, it must be at the heart of every other Christian virtue. Thus, for example, justice without love is legalism; faith without love is ideology; hope without love is self-centeredness; forgiveness without love is self-abasement; fortitude without love is recklessness; generosity without love is extravagance; care without love is mere duty; fidelity without love is servitude. Every virtue is an expression of love. No virtue is really a virtue unless it is permeated, or informed, by love.» - Richard Rohr

#310 «It doesn't matter who you are or what you look like, so long as somebody loves you.» - Roald Dahl

#311 «In love there are two things - bodies and words.» - Joyce Carol Oates

#312 «Of all forms of caution, caution in love is perhaps the most fatal to true happiness.» - Bertrand Russell

#313 «Love is not the absence of logic but logic examined and recalculated heated and curved to fit inside the contours of the heart.» - Tammara Webber

#314 «The lover is a monotheist who knows that other people worship different gods but cannot himself imagine that there could be other gods.» - Theodor Reik

#315 «But love's a malady without a cure.» - John Dryden

#316 «Don't beg anybody for anything, especially love.» - Toni Morrison

#317 «Peace of mind is another way of saying that you've learned how to love, that you have come to appreciate the importance of giving love in order to be worthy of receiving it.» - Hubert H. Humphrey

#318 «As long as you know men are like children, you know everything!» - Coco Chanel

#319 «I regard as a mortal sin not only the lying of the senses in matters of love, but also the illusion which the senses seek to create where love is only partial. I say, I believe, that one must love with all of one's being, or else live, come what may, a life of complete chastity.» - George Sand

#320 «Love is a dangerous angel.» - Francesca Lia Block

#321 «There is always some madness in love. But there is also always some reason in madness.» - Friedrich Nietzsche

#322 «Him that I love, I wish to be free -- even from me.» - Anne Morrow Lindbergh

#323 «If I say your voice is an amber waterfall in which I yearn to burn each day, if you eat my mouth like a mystical rose with powers of healing and damnation, If I confess that your body is the only civilization I long to experience... would it mean that we are close to knowing something about love?» - Aberjhani

#324 «True love doesn't come to you it has to be inside you.» - Julia Roberts

#325 «Love is something far more than desire for sexual intercourse; it is the principal means of escape from the loneliness which afflicts most men and women throughout the greater part of their lives.» - Bertrand Russell

#326 «The ultimate lesson all of us have to learn is unconditional love, which includes not only others but ourselves as well.» - Elisabeth Kubler-Ross

#327 «To him she seemed so beautiful, so seductive, so different from ordinary people, that he could not understand why no one was as disturbed as he by the clicking of her heels on the paving stones, why no one else's heart was wild with the breeze stirred by the sighs of her veils, why everyone did not go mad with the movements of her braid, the flight of her hands, the gold of her laughter. He had not missed a single one of her gestures, not one of the indications of her character, but he did not dare approach her for fear of destroying the spell.» - Gabriel Garcia Marquez

#328 «Love is the triumph of imagination over intelligence.» - H. L. Mencken

#329 «When two people relate to each other authentically and humanly, God is the electricity that surges between them.» - Martin Buber

#330 «Be careful of love. It'll twist your brain around and leave you thinking up is down and right is wrong.» - Rick Riordan

#331 «He who is devoid of the power to forgive is devoid of the power to love.» - Martin Luther King, Jr.

#332 «Never close your lips to those whom you have already opened your heart.» - Charles Dickens

#333 «And so let us always meet each other with a smile, for the smile is the beginning of love, and once we begin to love each other naturally we want to do something.» - Mother Teresa

#334 «I love her and that's the beginning and end of everything.» - F. Scott Fitzgerald

#335 «I will not be just a tourist in the world of images, just watching images passing by which I cannot live in, make love to, possess as permanent sources of joy and ecstasy.» - Anais Nin

#336 «Love is the force, the energy that animates creativity and peace in each one of us.» - Salle Merrill Redfield

#337 «Love, joy, and peace cannot flourish until you have freed yourself from mind dominance.» - Eckhart Tolle

#338 «The goal is to live in such a way that our lives will prove worth dying for... The one thing that can't be taken from us, even by death, is the love we give away before we go.» - Forrest Church

#339 «He is not a lover who does not love forever.» - Euripides

#340 «My lover asks me: "What is the difference between me and the sky?" The difference, my love, Is that when you laugh, I forget about the sky» - Nizar Qabbani

#341 «On this special day of love, remember that your Father loves you more than you could ever imagine...no matter what you've done or haven't done. No box of candy or flowers can compare to this kind of agape love!» - Joyce Meyer

#342 «If you keep in mind that love and love alone is the reason for living, it will calm your heart and free you from your worries.» - Harold Klemp

#343 «The only measure of your worth and your deeds will be the love you leave behind when you're gone.» - Fred Small

#344 «Life and love are life and love, a bunch of violets is a bunch of violets, and to drag in the idea of a point is to ruin everything. Live and let live, love and let love, flower and fade, and follow the natural curve, which flows on, pointless.» - D. H. Lawrence

#345 «Life is short. Kiss slowly, laugh insanely, love truly and forgive quickly» - Paulo Coelho

#346 «Be with me always - take any form - drive me mad! only do not leave me in this abyss, where I cannot find you! Oh, God! it is unutterable! I can not live without my life! I can not live without my soul!» - Emily Bronte

#347 «[...] each of us is born with a box of matches inside us but we can't strike them all by ourselves» - Laura Esquivel

#348 «Love is the child of illusion and the parent of disillusion.» - Miguel de Unamuno

#349 «Love blinds us to faults, hatred to virtues.» - Moses ibn Ezra

#350 «Where love is concerned, too much is not even enough.» - Pierre Beaumarchais

#351 «In love, unlike most other passions, the recollection of what you have had and lost is always better than what you can hope for in the future.» - Stendhal

#352 «For love is immortality.» - Emily Dickinson

#353 «We weren't meant to be somebody--we were meant to know Somebody» - John Piper

#354 «Eve was not taken out of Adam's head to top him, neither out of his feet to be trampled on by him, but out of his side to be equal with him, under his arm to be protected by him, and near his heart to be loved by him.» - Matthew Henry

#355 «Acquire the habit of speaking to God as if you were alone with Him, familiarly and with confidence and love, as to the dearest and most loving of friends.» - Alphonsus Liguori

#356 «Let no one believe that he has received the divine kiss, if he knows the truth without loving it or loves it without understanding it. But blessed is that kiss whereby not only is God recognized but also the Father is loved; for there is never full knowledge without perfect love.» - Bernard of Clairvaux

#357 «Do not waste time bothering whether you 'love' your neighbor; act as if you did. As soon as we do this we find one of the great secrets. When you are behaving as if you loved someone, you will presently come to love him.» - C. S. Lewis

#358 «Treasure the love you receive above all. It will survive long after your good health has vanished.» - Og Mandino

#359 «The real act of marriage takes place in the heart, not in the ballroom or church or synagogue. It's a choice you make on your wedding day, and over and over again and that choice is reflected in the way you treat your husband.» - Barbara De Angelis

#360 «Your heart is my piñata.» - Chuck Palahniuk

#361 «Love is that condition in which the happiness of another person is essential to your own.» - Robert A. Heinlein

#362 «Yesterday we obeyed kings and bent our necks before emperors. But today we kneel only to truth, follow only beauty, and obey only love.» - Khalil Gibran

#363 «If you live to be a hundred, I want to live to be a hundred minus one day so I never have to live without you.» - A. A. Milne

#364 «Anyone who tries to imprison love will cut off the spring that feeds it, and the trapped water will grow stagnant and rank.» - Paulo Coelho

#365 «Pray for the love which allows you to see the good in your companion. Pray for the love that makes weaknesses and mistakes seem small. Pray for the love to make your companion's joy your own. Pray for the love to want to lessen the load and soften the sorrows of your companion» - Henry B. Eyring

#366 «Life is very simple. What I give out comes back to me.
Today, I choose to give love.» - Louise Hay"

#367 «In bed my real love has always been the sleep that rescued me by allowing me to dream.» - Luigi Pirandello

#368 «There is a woman at the begining of all great things.» - Alphonse de Lamartine

#369 «What a man takes in by contemplation, that he pours out in love.» - Meister Eckhart

#370 «Because God has made us for Himself, our hearts are restless until they rest in Him.» - Saint Augustine

#371 «Love is always open arms. If you close your arms about love you will find that you are left holding only yourself.» - Leo Buscaglia

#372 «Happiness often sneaks in through a door you didn't know you left open.» - John Barrymore

#373 «Lord, make me an instrument of thy peace. Where there is hatred, let me sow love.» - Francis of Assisi

#374 «I am a hard person to love but when I love, I love really hard.» - Tupac Shakur

#375 «What woman says to fond lover should be written on air or the swift water.

[Lat., Mulier cupido quod dicit amanti,
In vento et rapida scribere oportet aqua.]» - Catullus"

#376 «When love is not madness, it is not love.» - Pedro Calderon de la Barca

#377 «God's Love is always working to help Soul find its way back home» - Harold Klemp

#378 «My debt to you, Belovèd,

Is one I cannot pay

In any coin of any realm

On any reckoning day.» - Jessie Belle Rittenhouse"

#379 «Snape's patronus was a doe,' said Harry, 'the same as my mother's because he loved her for nearly all of his life, from when they were children.» - J. K. Rowling

#380 «Don't forget I'm just a girl, standing in front of a boy, asking him to love her.» - Julia Roberts

#381 «You cannot make someone love you. All you can do is be someone who can be loved. The rest is up up them.» - H. Jackson Brown, Jr.

#382 «Yes, love indeed is light from heaven; A spark of that immortal fire with angels shared, by Allah given to lift from earth our low desire.» - Lord Byron

#383 «If the thing loved is base, the lover becomes base.» - Leonardo da Vinci

#384 «One may have a blazing hearth in one's soul and yet no one ever came to sit by it. Passers-by see only a wisp of smoke from the chimney and continue on their way.» - Vincent Van Gogh

#385 «Paradise is always where love dwells.» - Jean Paul

#386 «Love that well which thou must leave ere long.» - William Shakespeare

#387 «To love someone is to acknowledge the goodness of who they are. Through loving a person we awaken their awareness of their own innate goodness. It is as though they cannot know how worthy they are until they look into the mirror of our love and see themselves.» - John Gray

#388 «Love cures people - both the ones who give it and the ones who receive it.» - Karl A. Menninger

#389 «I love you. I am who I am because of you. You are every reason, every hope, and every dream I've ever had, and no matter what happens to us in the future, everyday we are together is the greatest day of my life. I will always be yours.» - Nicholas Sparks

#390 «There is no instinct like that of the heart.» - Lord Byron

#391 «Perhaps love is like a resting place, a shelter from the storm. It exists to give you comfort, it is there to keep you warm, and in those times of trouble when you are most alone, the memory of love will bring you home.» - John Denver

#392 «I was about half in love with her by the time we sat down. That's the thing about girls. Every time they do something pretty... you fall half in love with them, and then you never know where the hell you are.» - J. D. Salinger

#393 «Darkness cannot drive out darkness; only light can do that. Hate cannot drive out hate; only love can do that.» - Martin Luther King, Jr.

#394 «Welcome to the wonderful world of jealousy, he thought. For the price of admission, you get a splitting headache, a nearly irresistable urge to commit murder, and an inferiority complex. Yippee.» - J.R. Ward

#395 «We are shaped and fashioned by what we love» - Johann Wolfgang von Goethe

#396 «My true love hath my heart, and I have his» - Philip Sidney

#397 «I almost wish we were butterflies and liv'd but three summer days - three such days with you I could fill with more delight than fifty common years could ever contain.» - John Keats

#398 «We don't need to explain our love. We only need to show it.» - Paulo Coelho

#399 «Although the sovereignty of God is universal and absolute, it is not the sovereignty of blind power. It is coupled with infinite wisdom, holiness and love. And this doctrine, when properly understood, is a most comforting and reassuring one. Who would not prefer to have his affairs in the hands of a God of infinite power, wisdom, holiness and love, rather than to have them left to fate, or chance, or irrevocable natural law, or to short-sighted and perverted self? Those who reject God's sovereignty should consider what alternatives they have left.» - Loraine Boettner

#400 «If somebody says, "I love you," to me, I feel as though I had a pistol pointed at my head. What can anybody reply under such conditions but that which the pistol-holder requires? "I love you, too."« - Kurt Vonnegut

#401 «Each moment of a happy lover's hour is worth an age of dull and common life.» - Aphra Behn

#402 «The story of my recent life.' I like that phrase. It makes more sense than 'the story of my life', because we get so many lives between birth and death. A life to be a child. A life to come of age. A life to wander, to settle, to fall in love, to parent, to test our promise, to realize our mortality- and in some lucky cases, to do something after that realization.» - Mitch Albom

#403 «Have you ever been in love? Horrible isn't it? It makes you so vulnerable. It opens your chest and it opens up your heart and it means that someone can get inside you and mess you up.» - Neil Gaiman

#404 «The more familiar two people become, the more the language they speak together departs from that of the ordinary, dictionary-defined discourse. Familiarity creates a new language, an in-house language of intimacy that carries reference to the story the two lovers are weaving together and that cannot be readily understood by others.» - Alain de Botton

#405 «Son, brother, father, lover, friend. There is room in the heart for all the affections, as there is room in heaven for all the stars.» - Victor Hugo

#406 «Love is always being given where it is not required.» - E. M. Forster

#407 «Define yourself radically as one beloved by God. This is the true self. Every other identity is illusion.» - Brennan Manning

#408 «The power of a glance has been so much abused in love stories, that it has come to be disbelieved in. Few people dare now to say that two beings have fallen in love because they have looked at each other. Yet it is in this way that love begins, and in this way only.» - Victor Hugo

#409 «Only love can be divided endlessly and still not diminish.» - Anne Morrow Lindbergh

#410 «Love is the motivating principle by which the Lord leads us along the way towards becoming like Him, our perfect example. Our way of life, hour by hour, must be filled with the love of God and love for others.» - Henry B. Eyring

#411 «Love is the cheapest of religions.» - Cesare Pavese

#412 «Love is a game that two can play and both win.» - Eva Gabor

#413 «True love is like ghosts, which everyone talks about and few have seen.» - Francois de La Rochefoucauld

#414 «There is only one happiness in this life, to love and be loved.» - George Sand

#415 «Anyone who loves in the expectation of being loved in return is wasting their time.» - Paulo Coelho

#416 «All my life, my heart has yearned for a thing I cannot name.» - Andre Breton

#417 «People always say that, when you love someone, nothing in the world matters. But that's not true, is it? You know, and I know, that when you love someone, everything in the world matters a little bit more.» - Jodi Picoult

#418 «Love is the master key that opens the gates of happiness.» - Oliver Wendell Holmes Sr.

#419 «You don't love someone because they're perfect, you love them in spite of the fact that they're not.» - Jodi Picoult

#420 «"And what would humans be without love?" Rare, said Death.» - Terry Pratchett

#421 «Your life and my life flow into each other as wave flows into wave, and unless there is peace and joy and freedom for you, there can be no real peace or joy or freedom for me. To see reality-not as we expect it to be but as it is-is to see that unless we live for each other and in and through each other, we do not really live very satisfactorily; that there can really be life only where there really is, in just this sense, love.» - Frederick Buechner

#422 «Love of Allah is the power of the heart, the sustenance of the heart, the light of the heart.» - Ibn Qayyim Al-Jawziyya

#423 «One makes mistakes; that is life. But it is never a mistake to have loved.» - Romain Rolland

#424 «The hardest-learned lesson: that people have only their kind of love to give, not our kind.» - Mignon McLaughlin

#425 «Love rules the court, the camp, the grove, And men below, and saints above: For love is heaven, and heaven is love.» - Walter Scott

#426 «Love is the ultimate outlaw. It just won't adhere to any rules. The most any of us can do is sign on as its accomplice.» - Tom Robbins

#427 «If there is such a thing as a good marriage, it is because it resembles friendship rather than love.» - Michel de Montaigne

#428 «Whatever our souls are made of, his and mine are the same.» - Emily Bronte

#429 «Love does not consist in gazing at each other, but in looking outward together in the same direction.» - Antoine de Saint-Exupery

#430 «Listen to the inner light;
It will guide you.

Listen to the inner Peace;
It will feed you.

Listen to the inner Love;
It will transform you,

It will divinise you,
It will immortalise you.» - Sri Chinmoy"

#431 «Time is too slow for those who wait, too swift for those who fear, too long for those who grieve, too short for those who rejoice, but for those who love, time is eternity.» - Henry Van Dyke

#432 «Immature love says: 'I love you because I need you.' Mature love says 'I need you because I love you.'« - Erich Fromm

#433 «Beauty is not in the face; beauty is a light in the heart.» - Khalil Gibran

#434 «God has spoken to me many times that my job is to love and his job is to heal.» - Heidi Baker

#435 «Without you in my arms, I feel an emptiness in my soul. I find myself searching the crowds for your face - I know it's an impossibility, but I cannot help myself.» - Nicholas Sparks

#436 «Love... it surrounds every being and extends slowly to embrace all that shall be.» - Khalil Gibran

#437 «The story of human intimacy is one of constantly allowing ourselves to see those we love most deeply in a new, more fractured light. Look hard. Risk that.» - Cheryl Strayed

#438 «Let choice whisper in your ear and love murmur in your heart. Be ready. Here comes life.» - Maya Angelou

#439 «A woman can forgive a man for the harm he does her...but she can never forgive him for the sacrifices he makes on her account.» - W. Somerset Maugham

#440 «I haven't changed my mind. That's the point! I want to spend my life with you even though it's totally irrational. And you have short earlobes. Socially and genetically there's no reason for me to be attracted to you. The only logical conclusion is that I must be in love with you.» - Graeme Simsion

#441 «Great loves too must be endured.» - Coco Chanel

#442 «Love is just a word until someone comes along and gives it meaning.» - Paulo Coelho

#443 «Love takes up where knowledge leaves off.» - Thomas Aquinas

#444 «When desire, having rejected reason and overpowered judgment which leads to right, is set in the direction of the pleasure which beauty can inspire, and when again under the influence of its kindred desires it is moved with violent motion towards the beauty of corporeal forms, it acquires a surname from this very violent motion, and is called love.» - Socrates

#445 «Love isn't love until you give it away.» - Michael W. Smith

#446 «We grow great by dreams. All big men are dreamers. They see things in the soft haze of a spring day or in the red fire of a long winter's evening. Some of us let these great dreams die, but others nourish and protect them; nurse them through bad days till they bring them to the sunshine and light which comes always to those who sincerely hope that their dreams will come true.» - Woodrow Wilson

#447 «There is only one kind of love, but there are a thousand imitations.» - Francois de La Rochefoucauld

#448 «The present moment is always full of infinite treasure. It contains far more than you can possibly grasp. Faith is the measure of its riches: what you find in the present moment is according to the measure of your faith. Love also is the measure: the more the heart loves, the more it rejoices in what God provides. The will of God presents itself at each moment like an immense ocean that the desire of your heart cannot empty; yet you will drink from that ocean according to your faith and love.» - Jean-Pierre de Caussade

#449 «What's terrible is to pretend that second-rate is first-rate. To pretend that you don't need love when you do; or you like your work when you know quite well you're capable of better.» - Doris Lessing

#450 «A woman knows the face of the man she loves as a sailor knows the open sea.» - Honore de Balzac

#451 «Life will break you. Nobody can protect you from that. And living alone won't either, for solitude will also break you with its yearning. You have to love. You have to feel. It is the reason you are here on Earth.» - Louise Erdrich

#452 «Love, love, love - all the wretched cant of it, masking egotism, lust, masochism, fantasy under a mythology of sentimental postures.» - Germaine Greer

#453 «Happiness lies in a large measure of self-forgetfulness, either in work . . . or in the love of others. ♥» - Everett Ruess

#454 «There is no more lovely, friendly and charming relationship, communion or company than a good marriage.» - Martin Luther

#455 «The things we love destroy us every time, lad. Remember that.» - George R. R. Martin

#456 «If a person loves only one other person and is indifferent to all others, his love is not love but a symbiotic attachment, or an enlarged egotism.» - Erich Fromm

#457 «Love is an attempt at penetrating another being, but it can only succeed if the surrender is mutual.» - Octavio Paz

#458 «In real life, love has to be possible. Even if it is not returned right away, love can only survive when the hope exists that you will be able to win over the person you desire.» - Paulo Coelho

#459 «And in this game of life, we all search for ourselves. When I say selves, I mean 'inner selves', the thing that created the life in the first place. Now consciously, most of us are not aware of this. But if you're searching for happiness; if you're searching for tranquility; if you're searching just to have a nice, peaceful, loving, understanding life... in actual fact, your searching for your inner self.» - Sydney Banks

#460 «Love is life's end, but never ending. Love is life's wealth, never spent, but ever spending. Love's life's reward, rewarded in rewarding.» - Herbert Spencer

#461 «Real love is a permanently self-enlarging experience.» - M. Scott Peck

#462 «...the heart is an organ of fire.» - Michael Ondaatje

#463 «What does love look like? It has the hands to help others. It has the feet to hasten to the poor and needy. It has eyes to see misery and want. It has the ears to hear the sighs and sorrows of men. That is what love looks like.» - Saint Augustine

#464 «Love is not only something you feel, it is something you do.» - David Wilkerson

#465 «When you plant lettuce, if it does not grow well, you don't blame the lettuce. You look for reasons it is not doing well. It may need fertilizer, or more water, or less sun. You never blame the lettuce. Yet if we have problems with our friends or family, we blame the other person. But if we know how to take care of them, they will grow well, like the lettuce. Blaming has no positive effect at all, nor does trying to persuade using reason and arguments. That is my experience. No blame, no reasoning, no argument, just understanding.» - Nhat Hanh

#466 «The deeper that sorrow carves into your being, the more joy you can contain.» - Khalil Gibran

#467 «Happiness, that grand mistress of the ceremonies in the dance of life, impels us through all its mazes and meanderings, but leads none of us by the same route.» - Charles Caleb Colton

#468 «We never know the love of the parent for the child till we become parents.» - Henry Ward Beecher

#469 «For all sad words of tongue and pen, The saddest are these, 'It might have been'.» - John Greenleaf Whittier

#470 «Love life and life will love you back. Love people and they will love you back.» - Arthur Rubinstein

#471 «There is a courtesy of the heart; it is allied to love. From its springs the purest courtesy in the outward behavior.» - Johann Wolfgang von Goethe
#472 «When we are in love we seem to ourselves quite different from what we were before.» - Blaise Pascal

#473 «I believe that if I should die, and you were to walk near my grave, from the very depths of the earth I would hear your footsteps.» - Benito Perez Galdos

#474 «Love is when you don't have to be with another person to touch their heart!» - Torquato Tasso

#475 «What if you slept? And what if, in your sleep, you went to heaven and there plucked a strange and beautiful flower? And what if,when you awoke,you had the flower in your hand? Ah, what then?» - Samuel Taylor Coleridge

#476 «When I am with you, we stay up all night. When you're not here, I can't go to sleep. Praise God for those two insomnias! And the difference between them.» - Rumi

#477 «Love matches are made by people who are content, for a month of honey, to condemn themselves to a life of vinegar.» - Marguerite Gardiner, Countess of Blessington

#478 «The love we give away is the only love we keep.» - Elbert Hubbard

#479 «There is love enough in this world for everybody, if people will just look.» - Kurt Vonnegut

#480 «To love is to suffer. To avoid suffering one must not love. But then one suffers from not loving. Therefore, to love is to suffer; not to love is to suffer; to suffer is to suffer. To be happy is to love. To be happy, then, is to suffer, but suffering makes one unhappy. Therefore, to be happy one must love or love to suffer or suffer from too much happiness.» - Woody Allen

#481 «But true love is a durable fire, In the mind ever burning, Never sick, never old, never dead, From itself never turning.» - Walter Raleigh

#482 «Pleasure of love lasts but a moment, Pain of love lasts a lifetime.» - Bette Davis

#483 «Will you still love me when I'm a monster?» - Margaret Mahy

#484 «I never knew how to worship until I knew how to love.» - Henry Ward Beecher

#485 «Anyone can love a rose, but it takes a lot to love a leaf.» - Tom Flynn

#486 «The pain of love is the pain of being alive. It is a perpetual wound.» - Maureen Duffy

#487 «I like flaws. I think they make things interesting.» - Sarah Dessen

#488 «Joy attracts more joy. Happiness attracts more happiness. Peace attracts more peace. GRATITUDE attracts more GRATITUDE. Kindness attracts more kindness. Love attracts more love.

Your job is an inside one. To change your world, all you have to do is change the way you feel inside. How easy is that?» - Rhonda Byrne"

#489 «The only victory over love is flight.» - Napoleon Bonaparte

#490 «Ah, love, let us be true
To one another!» - Matthew Arnold"

#491 «The most powerful symptom of love is a tenderness which becomes at times almost insupportable.» - Victor Hugo

#492 «Love is a chain of love as nature is a chain of life.» - Truman Capote
#493 «The most precious gift we can offer anyone is our attention. When mindfulness embraces those we love, they will bloom like flowers.» - Nhat Hanh

#494 «True love blooms when we care more about another person than we care about ourselves. That is Christ's great atoning example for us, and it ought to be more evident in the kindness we show, the respect we give, and the selflessness and courtesy we employ in our personal relationships.» - Jeffrey R. Holland

#495 «I've been blessed. I have no complaints. I've been surrounded by people in radio, on stage and in motion pictures and television who love me. The things that have gone wrong have been simply physical things.» - Dick York

#496 «Oh, be wise, Thou!

Instructed that true knowledge leads to love.» - William Wordsworth"

#497 «For my part, I prefer my heart to be broken. It is so lovely, dawn-kaleidoscopic within the crack.» - D. H. Lawrence

#498 «It's not complicated. Just love the one in front of you.» - Heidi Baker

#499 «When I saw you I fell in love. And you smiled because you knew.» - Arrigo Boito

#500 «Love consists in this, that two solitudes protect and touch and greet each other.» - Rainer Maria Rilke

#501 «We shouldn't pray for a lighter load to carry but a stronger back to endure! Then the world will see that God is with us, empowering us to live in a way that reflects his love and power.» - Brother Yun

#502 «If you judge people, you have no time to love them.» - Mother Teresa

#503 «The loving personality seeks not to control, but to nurture, not to dominate, but to empower.» - Gary Zukav

#504 «I get that you're scared and that you've been hurt. But doing what is easy and safe is no way to live, and a life without passion and love is so far beneath what you deserve.» - Kiersten White

#505 «The sweet love between the moon and the deep blue sea.» - Jimi Hendrix

#506 «Where there's marriage without love, there will be love without marriage.» - Benjamin Franklin

#507 «But love is blind and lovers cannot see» - William Shakespeare

#508 «Love is like those second-rate hotels where all the luxury is in the lobby.» - Paul-Jean Toulet

#509 «Life began after I fell in love with you» - Brad Hodge

#510 «Follow love and it will flee, flee love and it will follow thee.» - John Gay

#511 «Passion makes the world go round. Love just makes it a safer place.» - Ice T

#512 «He felt now that he was not simply close to her, but that he did not know where he ended and she began.» - Leo Tolstoy

#513 «We conceal it from ourselves in vain - we must always love something. In those matters seemingly removed from love, the feeling is secretly to be found, and man cannot possibly live for a moment without it.» - Blaise Pascal

#514 «Happy is love or friendship when returned-- The lovers whose pure flames have equal burned.» - Bion of Smyrna

#515 «I am nothing special, of this I am sure. I am a common man with common thoughts and I've led a common life. There are no monuments dedicated to me and my name will soon be forgotten, but I've loved another with all my heart and soul, and to me, this has always been enough.» - Nicholas Sparks

#516 «Come live with me and be my love, And we will all the pleasures prove, That valleys, groves, hills, and fields, Woods, or steepy mountain yields.» - Christopher Marlowe

#517 «Love is an unconditional commitment to an imperfect person.» - Selwyn Hughes

#518 «I have so much of you in my heart.» - John Keats

#519 «I will greet this day with love in my heart. And how will I do this? Henceforth will I look on all things with love and be born again. I will love the sun for it warms my bones; yet I will love the rain for it cleanses my spirit. I will love the light for it shows me the way; yet I will love the darkness for it shows me the stars. I will welcome happiness as it enlarges my heart; yet I will endure sadness for it opens my soul. I will acknowledge rewards for they are my due; yet I will welcome obstacles for they are my challenge.» - Og Mandino

#520 «Love must be learned and learned again; There is no end.» - Katherine Anne Porter

#521 «Love should be a tree whose roots are deep in the earth, but whose branches extend into heaven.» - Bertrand Russell

#522 «We can recognize the dawn and the decline of love by the uneasiness we feel when alone together.» - Jean de la Bruyere

#523 «Love the moment and the energy of that moment will spread beyond all boundaries.» - Corita Kent

#524 «The sound of a kiss is not so loud as that of a cannon, but its echo lasts a great deal longer.» - Oliver Wendell Holmes Sr.

#525 «Stand by your man. Give him two arms to cling to and something warm to come to.» - Tammy Wynette

#526 «The closer I'm bound in love to you, the closer I am to free.» - Robert Green Ingersoll
#527 «If you are not long, I will wait for you all my life.» - Oscar Wilde

#528 «The most wonderful of all things in life is the discovery of another human being with whom one's relationship has a growing depth, beauty and joy as the years increase. This inner progressiveness of love between two human beings is a most marvelous thing; it cannot be found by looking for it or by passionately wishing for it. It is a sort of divine accident, and the most wonderful of all things in life.» - Hugh Walpole

#529 «There's a reason we are drawn to the light. A reason why we fear darkness. It's important to be terrified and unnerved about certain things. That way we will choose another path. The path that leads us to truth and love.» - Ted Dekker

#530 «For a crowd is not company; and faces are but a gallery of pictures; and talk but a tinkling cymbal, where there is no love.» - Francis Bacon

#531 «The human heart is a strange vessel. Love and hatred can exist side by side.» - Scott Westerfeld

#532 «True love begins when nothing is looked for in return.» - Antoine de Saint-Exupery

#533 «I am not sure exactly what heaven will be like, but I know that when we die and it comes time for God to judge us, he will not ask, 'How many good things have you done in your life?' rather he will ask, 'How much love did you put into what you did?'« - Mother Teresa

#534 «My soul gave me good counsel, teaching me to love. Love was for me a delicate thread stretched between two adjacent pegs, but now it has been transformed into a halo, its first is its last, and its last is its first. It encompasses every being, slowly expanding to embrace all that ever will be.» - Rumi

#535 «Love, you are eternal like springtime.» - Juan Ramon Jimenez

#536 «Love is like a brick. You can build a house, or you can sink a dead body.» - Lady Gaga

#537 «A warrior so bold, and a virgin so bright,
Conversed as they sat on the green.

They gazed on each other with tender delight,
Alonzo the Brave was the name of the knight--

The maiden's the Fair Imogene.» - Matthew Gregory Lewis"

#538 «Are you ready to cut off your head and place your foot on it? If so, come; Love awaits you! Love is not grown in a garden, nor sold in the marketplace; whether you are a king or a servant, the price is your head, and nothing less. Yes, the cost of the elixir of love is your head! Do you hesitate? 0 miser, It is cheap at that price!» - Al-Ghazali

#539 «Don't waste your love on somebody, who doesn't value it.» - William Shakespeare

#540 «We loved with a love that was more than love.» - Edgar Allan Poe

#541 «And when my own Mark Antony
Against young Caesar strove,

And Rome's whole world was set in arms,
The cause was,--all for love.» - Robert Southey"

#542 «I am in you and you in me, mutual in divine love.» - William Blake

#543 «It is love, not reason, that is stronger than death.» - Thomas Mann

#544 «In the end, the love you take is equal to the love you make.» - Paul McCartney
#545 «A hug is like a boomerang - you get it back right away.» - Bil Keane

#546 «A good marriage is where both people feel like they're getting the better end of the deal.» - Anne Lamott

#547 «Love is a portion of the soul itself, and it is of the same nature as the celestial breathing of the atmosphere of paradise.» - Victor Hugo

#548 «Friendship at first sight, like love at first sight, is said to be the only truth.» - Herman Melville

#549 «For life, with all its yields of joy and woe Is just a chance o' the prize of learning love.» - Robert Browning

#550 «The giving of love and understanding is an education in itself.» - Eleanor Roosevelt

#551 «We look forward to the time when the Power of Love will replace the Love of Power. Then will our world know the blessings of peace.» - William E. Gladstone

#552 «Love grows by giving. The love we give away is the only love we keep. The only way to retain love is to give it away.» - Elbert Hubbard

#553 «Love loves to love love.» - James Joyce

#554 «Perhaps all the dragons in our lives are princesses who are only waiting to see us act, just once, with beauty and courage. Perhaps everything that frightens us is, in its deepest essence, something helpless that wants our love.» - Rainer Maria Rilke

#555 «Politics is for the present, but an equation is for eternity.» - Albert Einstein

#556 «Sometimes when you look back on a situation, you realize it wasn't all you thought it was. A beautiful girl walked into your life. You fell in love. Or did you? Perhaps, it was only a childish infatuation, or maybe just a brief moment of vanity.» - Henry Bromell

#557 «The mark of a true crush... is that you fall in love first and grope for reasons afterward.» - Shana Alexander

#558 «Love lodged in a woman's breast is but a guest.» - Henry Wotton

#559 «Remember that the best relationship is one in which your love for each other exceeds your need for each other.» - Dalai Lama

#560 «You know, when it works, love is pretty amazing. It's not overrated. There's a reason for all those songs.» - Sarah Dessen

#561 «Love is all we have, the only way that each can help the other.» - Euripides

#562 «No one can love you until you love yourself, and you cannot love anyone else, until you love yourself.» - Raymond Charles Barker

#563 «Love is of all passions the strongest, for it attacks simultaneously the head, the heart and the senses.» - Laozi

#564 «Some people never say the words 'I love you', for like a child they're longing to be told.» - Paul Simon

#565 «Nothing can be loved or hated unless it is first known.» - Leonardo da Vinci

#566 «When all of your wishes are granted, many of your dreams will be destroyed.» - Marilyn Manson

#567 «Love is like the measles; we all have to go through it.» - Jerome K. Jerome

#568 «The hours I spend with you I look upon as sort of a perfumed garden, a dim twilight, and a fountain singing to it. You and you alone make me feel that I am alive. Other men it is said have seen angels, but I have seen thee and thou art enough.» - George Edward Moore

#569 «Love is the only reality and it is not a mere sentiment. It is the ultimate truth that lies at the heart of creation.» - Rabindranath Tagore

#570 «Love is like quicksilver in the hand. Leave the fingers open and it stays. Clutch it and it darts away.» - Dorothy Parker

#571 «What a man calls his 'conscience' is merely the mental action that follows a sentimental reaction after too much wine or love.» - Helen Rowland

#572 «Until then, mio dolce amor, a thousand kisses; but give me none in return, for they set my blood on fire.» - Napoleon Bonaparte

#573 «Traveling in the company of those we love is home in motion.» - Leigh Hunt

#574 «Life without love is like a tree without blossoms or fruit." "Love has no other desire but to fulfill itself. To melt and be like a running brook that sings its melody to the night. To wake at dawn with a winged heart and give thanks for another day of loving» - Khalil Gibran

#575 «There is no difficulty that enough love will not conquer: no disease that love will not heal: no door that enough love will not open...It makes no difference how deep set the trouble: how hopeless the outlook: how muddled the tangle: how great the mistake. A sufficient realization of love will dissolve it all. If only you could love enough you would be the happiest and most powerful being in the world.» - Emmet Fox

#576 «When you heart is ablaze with the love of God, when you love other people - especially the ripsnorting sinners - so much that you dare to tell them about Jesus with no apologies, then never fear, there will be results.» - Catherine Marshall

#577 «Beauty is when you can appreciate yourself. When you love yourself, that's when you're most beautiful.» - Zoe Kravitz

#578 «Ask not of me, love, what is love?

Ask what is good of God above;
Ask of the great sun what is light;

Ask what is darkness of the night;

Ask sin of what may be forgiven;

Ask what is happiness of heaven;
Ask what is folly of the crowd;

Ask what is fashion of the shroud;
Ask what is sweetness of thy kiss;

Ask of thyself what beauty is.» - Philip James Bailey"

#579 «No one can understand love who has not experienced infatuation. And no one can understand infatuation, no matter how many times he has experienced it.» - Mignon McLaughlin

#580 «For one human being to love another; that is perhaps the most difficult of all our tasks, the ultimate, the last test and proof, the work for which all other work is but preparation.» - Rainer Maria Rilke

#581 «Women are often under the impression that men are much more madly in love with them than they really are.» - W. Somerset Maugham

#582 «If there's a thing I've learned in my life it's to not be afraid of the responsibility that comes with caring for other people. What we do for love: those things endure. Even if the people you do them for don't» - Cassandra Clare

#583 «You are as prone to love, as the sun is to shine.» - Thomas Traherne

#584 «Love is not automatic. It takes conscious practice and awareness, just like playing the piano or golf. However, you have ample opportunities to practice. Everyone you meet can be your practice session.» - Hari

#585 «Love is the medicine of all moral evil. By it the world is to be cured of sin.» - Henry Ward Beecher

#586 «If you love deeply, you're going to get hurt badly. But it's still worth it.» - C. S. Lewis

#587 «For every beauty there is an eye somewhere to see it. For every truth there is an ear somewhere to hear it. For every love there is a heart somewhere to receive it.» - Ivan Panin

#588 «Love expects no reward. Love knows no fear. Love Divine gives - does not demand. Love thinks no evil; imputes no motive. To Love is to share and serve.» - Sivananda

#589 «Will you love me in December as you do in May,
Will you love me in the good old fashioned way?
When my hair has all turned gray,

Will you kiss me then and say,

That you love me in December as you do in May?» - Jimmy Walker"

#590 «It seems everyone's so worried about getting hurt that they forget about letting love happen.» - Carlos Salinas

#591 «Do you wish to be free? Then above all things, love God, love your neighbor, love one another, love the common weal; then you will have true liberty.» - Girolamo Savonarola

#592 «Before I built a wall I'd ask to know what I was walling in or walling out.» - Robert Frost

#593 «Trust your heart if the seas catch fire, live by love though the stars walk backward.» - e. e. cummings

#594 «The truth of truths is love.» - Philip James Bailey

#595 «If you press me to say why I loved him, I can say no more than it was because he was he, and I was I.» - Michel de Montaigne

#596 «Ah love is bitter and sweet,
but which is more sweet

the bitterness or the sweetness,
none has spoken it.» - Hilda Doolittle"

#597 «Ah me! love can not be cured by herbs.

[Lat., Hei mihi! quod nullis amor est medicabilis herbis.]» -
Ovid"

#598 «A kiss makes the heart young again and wipes out
the years.» - Rupert Brooke

#599 «I really don't know what "I love you" means. I think
it means "Don't leave me here alone.» - Neil Gaiman

#600 «The love that moves the sun and the other stars.» -
Elizabeth Gilbert

#601 «Man may have discovered fire, but women
discovered how to play with it.» - Candace Bushnell

#602 «Love is the voice under all silences, the hope which
has no opposite in fear; the strength so strong mere force
is feebleness: the truth more first than sun, more last than
star.» - e. e. cummings

#603 «True love comes quietly, without banners or flashing lights. If you hear bells, get your ears checked.» - Erich Segal

#604 «Love and desire are the spirit's wings to great deeds.» - Johann Wolfgang von Goethe

#605 «People should fall in love with their eyes closed.» - Andy Warhol

#606 «There is nothing more important in life than love.» - Barbra Streisand

#607 «Love begins with a smile, grows with a kiss, and ends with a teardrop.» - Saint Augustine

#608 «Your work is going to fill a large part of your life, and the only way to be truly satisfied is to do what you believe is great work. And the only way to do great work is to love what you do. If you haven't found it yet, keep looking. Don't settle. As with all matters of the heart, you'll know when you find it.» - Steve Jobs

#609 «There is a close relationship between a house full of possessions and a heart full of desires, between a cluttered closet and a crowded schedule, between having no place to put possessions and having no priorities for our life. These are precious clues. They remind us to slow down, to live in the present, to reduce the desires that drain our vitality, to clarify priorities so we can give our time and attention to what matters most. Tragically, in the press of modern life, we have managed to get backwards one of life's most vital truths: people are to be loved; things are to be used.» - Eknath Easwaran

#610 «All, everything that I understand, I understand only because I love.» - Leo Tolstoy

#611 «Love cannot be reduced to a catalogue of reasons why, and a catalogue of reasons cannot be put together into love.» - Eleanor Catton

#612 «For small creatures such as we the vastness is bearable only through love.» - Carl Sagan

#613 «O love, O fire! once he drew With one long kiss my whole soul through My lips, as sunlight drinketh dew.» - Alfred Lord Tennyson

#614 «Gestures, in love, are incomparably more attractive, effective and valuable than words.» - Francois Rabelais

#615 «It is easier to hide behind philosophical arguments, heavily footnoted for effect, than it is to admit our hurts, our confusions, our loves, and our passions in the marketplace of life's heartfelt transactions.» - Ravi Zacharias

#616 «Do you want me to tell you something really subversive? Love is everything it's cracked up to be. That's why people are so cynical about it. It really is worth fighting for, being brave for, risking everything for. And the trouble is, if you don't risk anything, you risk even more.» - Erica Jong

#617 «Love is when you meet someone who tells you something new about yourself.» - Andre Breton

#618 «Love feels no burden, regards not labors, strives toward more than it attains, argues not of impossibility, since it believes that it may and can do all things.» - Thomas a Kempis

#619 «Because you speak to me in words, and I look at you with feelings.» - Anna Karina

#620 «For you was I born, for you do I have life, for you will I die, for you am I now dying.» - Gabriel Garcia Marquez

#621 «If I had a flower for every time I thought of you...I could walk through my garden forever.» - Alfred Lord Tennyson

#622 «Humanity I love you because when you're hard up you pawn your intelligence to buy a drink.» - e. e. cummings

#623 «You are the sunshine of my life! Thanks for brightening my world with the warmth of your Love.» - Jennie Garth

#624 «If you get down and quarell everyday, you're saying prayers to the devil, I say.» - Bob Marley

#625 «The more we love our friends, the less we flatter them; it is by excusing nothing that pure love shows itself.» - Moliere

#626 «When love and skill work together, expect a masterpiece.» - John Ruskin

#627 «We waste time looking for the perfect lover, instead of creating the perfect love.» - Tom Robbins

#628 «We pardon to the extent that we love.» - Francois de La Rochefoucauld

#629 «Love knows how to form itself. God will do his work if we do ours. Our job is to prepare ourselves for love. When we do, love finds us every time.» - Marianne Williamson

#630 «You are like nobody since I love you.» - Pablo Neruda

#631 «But when a young lady is to be a heroine, the perverseness of forty surrounding families cannot prevent her. Something must and will happen to throw a hero in her way.» - Jane Austen

#632 «All is love...All is love. With love comes understanding. With understanding comes patience. And then time stops. And everything is now.» - Brian Weiss

#633 «True love is rare, and it's the only thing that gives life real meaning.» - Nicholas Sparks

#634 «One, remember to look up at the stars and not down at your feet. Two, never give up work. Work gives you meaning and purpose and life is empty without it. Three, if you are lucky enough to find love, remember it is there and don't throw it away.» - Stephen Hawking

#635 «Who would give a law to lovers? Love is unto itself a higher law.» - Boethius

#636 «Love sucks. Sometimes it feels good. Sometimes it's just another way to bleed.» - Laurell K. Hamilton

#637 «You know how they say you only hurt the ones you love? Well, it works both ways.» - Chuck Palahniuk

#638 «Love is the only flower that grows and blossoms without the aid of the seasons» - Khalil Gibran

#639 «To love another person is to see the face of God.» - Victor Hugo

#640 «Our culture has accepted two huge lies. The first is that if you disagree with someone's lifestyle, you must fear or hate them. The second is that to love someone means you agree with everything they believe or do. Both are nonsense. You don't have to compromise convictions to be compassionate.» - Rick Warren

#641 «What is Love? Listen! It is the rainbow that stands out, in all its glorious many-colored hues, illuminating and making glad again the dark clouds of life. It is the morning and the evening star, that in glad refulgence, there on the awed horizon, call Nature's hearts to an uplifted rejoicing in God's marvelous firmament!» - Sinclair Lewis

#642 «On the last analysis, then, love is life. Love never faileth and life never faileth so long as there is love.» - Henry Drummond

#643 «How many times do I love, again?
Tell me how many beads there are

In a silver chain
Of evening rain

Unravelled from the trembling main
And threading the eye of a yellow star:-

So many times do I love again.» - Thomas Lovell Beddoes"

#644 «Neither a lofty degree of intelligence nor imagination nor both together go to the making of genius. Love, love, love, that is the soul of genius.» - Wolfgang Amadeus Mozart

#645 «This is the true measure of love, When we believe that we alone can love, That no one could ever have loved so before us, And that no one will ever love in the same way after us.» - Johann Wolfgang von Goethe

#646 «We need to teach the next generation of children from day one that they are responsible for their lives. Mankind's greatest gift, also its greatest curse, is that we have free choice. We can make our choices built from love or from fear.» - Elisabeth Kubler-Ross

#647 «When you love there is no 'I', so you cannot say 'I love you', only love is.» - Ivan Rados

#648 «Love is a conflict between reflexes and reflections.» - Magnus Hirschfeld

#649 «Could you imagine how horrible things would be if we always told others how we felt? Life would be intolerably bearable.» - R. K. Milholland

#650 «Some say that true love is a mirage; seek it anyway, for all else is surely desert.» - Robert Breault

#651 «Women hope men will change after marriage but they don't; men hope women won't change but they do.» - Bettina Arndt

#652 «The best proof of love is trust.» - Joyce Brothers

#653 «Children who are respected learn respect. Children who are cared for learn to care for those weaker than themselves. Children who are loved for what they are cannot learn intolerance. In an environment such as this, they will develop their own ideals, which can be nothing other than humane, since they grew out of the experience of love.» - Alice Miller

#654 «Two minds with but a single thought, two hearts that beat as one.» - Jasper Fforde

#655 «We are most alive when we're in love.» - John Updike

#656 «Love him and let him love you. Do you think anything else under heaven really matters?» - James A. Baldwin

#657 «and he suddenly knew that if she killed herself, he would die. Maybe not immediately, maybe not with the same blinding rush of pain, but it would happen. You couldn't live for very long without a heart.» - Jodi Picoult

#658 «Dumbledore watched her fly away, and as her silvery glow faded he turned back to Snape, and his eyes were full of tears. "After all this time?" "Always," said Snape.» - J. K. Rowling

#659 «Our culture says that feelings of love are the basis for actions of love. And of course that can be true. But it is truer to say that actions of love can lead consistently to feelings of love.» - Timothy Keller

#660 «There is no formula for generating the authentic warmth of love...Everyone has love, but it can only come out when he is convinced of the impossibility and frustration of trying to love himself. This conviction will not come through condemnations, through hating oneself, through calling self-love bad names in the universe. It comes only in the awareness that one has no self to love.» - Shunryu Suzuki

#661 «The man is a success who has lived well, laughed often, and loved much; who has gained the respect of intelligent men and the love of children; who has filled his niche and accomplished his task; who leaves the world better than he found it, whether by an improved poppy, a perfect poem, or a rescued soul; who never lacked appreciation of earth's beauty or failed to express it; who looked for the best in others and gave the best he had.» - Robert Louis Stevenson

#662 «There is no friendship, no love, like that of the parent for the child.» - Henry Ward Beecher

#663 «We love peace, as we abhor pusillanimity; but not peace at any price.» - Douglas William Jerrold
#664 «Sweet is true love that is given in vain, and sweet is death that takes away pain.» - Alfred Lord Tennyson

#665 «I am weird, you are weird. Everyone in this world is weird. One day two people come together in mutual weirdness and fall in love.» - Dr. Seuss

#666 «When you love someone, you love the person as they are, and not as you'd like them to be.» - Leo Tolstoy

#667 «New Yorkers love it when you spill your guts out there. Spill your guts at Wimbledon and they make you stop and clean it up.» - Jimmy Connors

#668 «The people will come and go. Sometimes they'll be there for you. Sometimes they wont. Some will love you, some will not. This tide was never meant to be still. Step away from time to time. And know that only a heart fixed on the unmoving spot can ride the waves of this ever-changing, ever-fading life.» - Yasmin Mogahed

#669 «I think you still love me, but we can't escape the fact that I'm not enough for you. I knew this was going to happen. So I'm not blaming you for falling in love with another woman. I'm not angry, either. I should be, but I'm not. I just feel pain. A lot of pain. I thought I could imagine how much this would hurt, but I was wrong.» - Haruki Murakami

#670 «What I need is the dandelion in the spring. The bright yellow that means rebirth instead of destruction. The promise that life can go on, no matter how bad our losses. That it can be good again.» - Suzanne Collins

#671 «Do you love me because I'm beautiful, or am I beautiful because you love me?» - Oscar Hammerstein II

#672 «As if you were on fire from within. The moon lives in the lining of your skin.» - Pablo Neruda

#673 «Every one of us is, in the cosmic perspective, precious. If a human disagrees with you, let him live. In a hundred billion galaxies, you will not find another.» - Carl Sagan

#674 «Alas! is even love too weak To unlock the heart, and let it speak?» - Matthew Arnold

#675 «By night, Love, tie your heart to mine, and the two together in their sleep will defeat the darkness» - Pablo Neruda

#676 «Love, I've come to understand, is more than three words mumbled before bedtime.» - Nicholas Sparks

#677 «I cannot fix on the hour, or the spot, or the look or the words, which laid the foundation. It is too long ago. I was in the middle before I knew that I had begun.» - Jane Austen

#678 «Love is also like a coconut which is good while it is fresh, but you have to spit it out when the juice is gone, what's left tastes bitter.» - Bertolt Brecht

#679 «When you love someone, you say their name different. Like it's safe inside your mouth.» - Jodi Picoult

#680 «Respect was invented to cover the empty place where love should be.» - Leo Tolstoy

#681 «Even during the worst hardships, when the other things in our lives seem to fall apart, we can still find peace in the eternal love of God.» - Armstrong Williams

#682 «Body is purified by water. Ego by tears. Intellect is purified by knowledge. And soul is purified with love.» - Ali ibn Abi Talib

#683 «I see love in black and white. Passion in shades of "gris". But when it comes to you and I, color is all I see.» - Lady Gaga

#684 «True love cannot be found where it does not exist, nor can it be denied where it does.» - Torquato Tasso

#685 «It makes no difference how deeply seated may be the trouble, how hopeless the outlook how muddled the tangle, how great the mistake. A sufficient realization of love will dissolve it all.» - Emmet Fox

#686 «Relationships become rocky when men and women fail to acknowledge they are biologically different and when each expects the other to live up to their expectations. Much of the stress we experience in relationships comes from the false belief that men and women are now the same and have the same priorities, drives and desires» - Barbara Pease

#687 «I'm in love with you," he said quietly. "Augustus," I said. "I am," he said. He was staring at me, and I could see the corners of his eyes crinkling. "I'm in love with you, and I'm not in the business of denying myself the simple pleasure of saying true things. I'm in love with you, and I know that love is just a shout into the void, and that oblivion is inevitable, and that we're all doomed and that there will come a day when all our labor has been returned to dust, and I know the sun will swallow the only earth we'll ever have, and I am in love with you.» - John Green

#688 «What a grand thing, to be loved! What a grander thing still, to love!» - Victor Hugo

#689 «Who is wise in love, love most, say least.» - Alfred Lord Tennyson

#690 «All you need is love. But a little chocolate now and then doesn't hurt.» - Charles M. Schulz

#691 «Love looks not with the eyes, but with the mind, And therefore is winged Cupid painted blind.» - William Shakespeare

#692 «It is the same in love as in war; a fortress that parleys is half taken.» - Margaret of Valois

#693 «beginnings are usually scary, and endings are usually sad, but its everything in between that makes it all worth living.» - Bob Marley

#694 «Love makes everything that is heavy light.» - Thomas a Kempis

#695 «One love, one heart, one destiny.» - Bob Marley

#696 «When I listen to love, I am listening to my true nature. When I express love, I am expressing my true nature» - Julia Cameron

#697 «It's a mistake to think that we have to be lovely to be loved by human beings or by God» - Fred Rogers

#698 «Every time a friend succeeds, I die a little.» - Gore Vidal

#699 «A man can be happy with any woman, as long as he does not love her.» - Oscar Wilde

#700 «What is Love? It is that powerful attraction towards all that we conceive, or fear, or hope beyond ourselves.» - Percy Bysshe Shelley

#701 «The quarrels of lovers are the renewal of love.» - Jean Racine

#702 «How sweet it is to love, and to be dissolved, and as it were to bathe myself in thy love.» - Thomas a Kempis

#703 «I love you as you are, but do not tell me how that is.» - Antonio Porchia

#704 «The only thing more unthinkable than leaving was staying; the only thing more impossible than staying was leaving.» - Elizabeth Gilbert

#705 «Reason is powerless in the expression of Love.» - Rumi

#706 «Love never reasons, but profusely gives,
Gives, like a thoughtless prodigal, its all,
And trembles then, lest it has done too little.» - Hannah More"

#707 «If you loved someone, you loved him, and when you had nothing else to give, you still gave him love.» - George Orwell

#708 «The more you love, the more you can love--and the more intensely you love. Nor is there any limit on how many you can love. If a person had time enough, he could love all of that majority who are decent and just.» - Robert A. Heinlein

#709 «And the trouble is, if you don't risk anything, you risk even more.» - Erica Jong

#710 «You are, and always have been, my dream.» - Nicholas Sparks

#711 «The love that lasts longest is the love that is never returned.» - W. Somerset Maugham

#712 «If you would be loved, love, and be loveable.» - Benjamin Franklin

#713 «the mind has a thousand eyes, and the heart has one:yet the light of a whole life dies when love is done.» - Daniel Handler

#714 «Love feels no burden, thinks nothing of trouble, attempts what is above its strength.... It is therefore able to undertake all things, and it completes many things, and warrants them to take effect, where he who does not love would faint and lie down.» - Thomas a Kempis

#715 «The human heart, at whatever age, opens to the heart that opens in return.» - Maria Edgeworth

#716 «Give us, O God, the vision which can see Your love in the world in spite of human failure. Give us the faith to trust Your goodness in spite of our ignorance and weakness. Give us the knowledge that we may continue to pray with understanding hearts. And show us what each one of us can do to set forward the coming of the day of universal peace.» - Frank Borman

#717 «While God waits for His temple to be built of love, men bring stones.» - Rabindranath Tagore

#718 «There is more pleasure in loving than in being beloved.» - Thomas Fuller

#719 «Love's gift cannot be given, it waits to be accepted.» - Rabindranath Tagore

#720 «Selfishness is one of the qualities apt to inspire love.» - Nathaniel Hawthorne

#721 «There is no difficulty that enough love will not conquer.» - Emmet Fox

#722 «I have always loved truth so passionately that I have often resorted to lying as a way of introducing it into the minds which were ignorant of its charms.» - Giacomo Casanova

#723 «Love for the joy of loving, and not for the offerings of someone else's heart.» - Marlene Dietrich

#724 «Till I loved I never lived.» - Emily Dickinson

#725 «Duty makes us do things well, but love makes us do them beautifully.» - Zig Ziglar

#726 «I love thee, I love thee with a love that shall not die. Till the sun grows cold and the stars grow old.» - William Shakespeare

#727 «The heart has its reasons of which reason knows nothing.» - Blaise Pascal

#728 «Friendship often ends in love, but love in friendship - never.» - Charles Caleb Colton

#729 «Chains do not hold a marriage together. It is threads, hundreds of tiny threads, which sew people together through the years.» - Simone Signoret

#730 «But I, being poor, have only my dreams; I have spread my dreams under your feet; Tread softly because you tread on my dreams.» - William Butler Yeats

#731 «I believe that two people are connected at the heart, and it doesn't matter what you do, or who you are or where you live; there are no boundaries or barriers if two people are destined to be together.» - Julia Roberts

#732 «I'm so in love, every time I look at you my soul gets dizzy.» - Jesse Tyler Ferguson

#733 «The lover knows much more about absolute good and universal beauty than any logician or theologian, unless the latter, too, be lovers in disguise.» - George Santayana

#734 «Love makes your soul crawl out from its hiding place.» - Zora Neale Hurston

#735 «Love and compassion are necessities, not luxuries. Without them humanity cannot survive.» - Dalai Lama

#736 «If she's amazing, she won't be easy. If she's easy, she won't be amazing. If she's worth it, you wont give up. If you give up, you're not worthy. ... Truth is, everybody is going to hurt you; you just gotta find the ones worth suffering for.» - Bob Marley

#737 «Things we lose have a way of coming back to us in the end, if not always in the way we expect.» - J. K. Rowling

#738 «Let there be spaces in your togetherness» - Khalil Gibran

#739 «Loving can cost a lot but not loving always costs more, and those who fear to love often find that want of love is an emptiness that robs the joy from life.» - Merle Shain

#740 «God, from a beautiful necessity, is Love.» - Martin Farquhar Tupper

#741 «Love is energy of life.» - Robert Browning

#742 «Men are from Earth, women are from Earth. Deal with it.» - George Carlin

#743 «Sometimes when I'm alone, I take the pearl from where it lives in my pocket and try to remember the boy with the bread, the strong arms that warded off nightmares on the train, the kisses in the arena.» - Suzanne Collins

#744 «O tyrant love, when held by you,
We may to prudence bid adieu.

[Fr., Amour! Amour! quand tu nous tiens
On peut bien dire, Adieu, prudence.]» - Jean de La Fontaine"

#745 «Love has no other desire but to fulfill itself.» - Khalil Gibran

#746 «Nobody has ever measured, not even poets, how much the heart can hold.» - Zelda Fitzgerald

#747 «I love everything that's old, - old friends, old times, old manners, old books, old wine.» - Oliver Goldsmith

#748 «A woman in love can't be reasonable - or she probably wouldn't be in love.» - Mae West

#749 «Being deeply loved by someone gives you strength, while loving someone deeply gives you courage.» - Laozi

#750 «You are as prone to love as the sun is to shine; it being the most delightful and natural employment of the soul of humans.» - Thomas Traherne

#751 «I've never fooled anyone. I've let people fool themselves. They didn't bother to find out who and what I was. Instead they would invent a character for me. I wouldn't argue with them. They were obviously loving somebody I wasn't.» - Marilyn Monroe

#752 «If you find someone you love in your life, then hang on to that love.» - Princess Diana

#753 «Keep love in your heart. A life without it is like a sunless garden when the flowers are dead.» - Oscar Wilde

#754 «I can feel Peeta press his forehead into my temple and he asks, 'So now that you've got me, what are you going to do with me?' I turn into him. 'Put you somewhere you can't get hurt.» - Suzanne Collins

#755 «Love me when I least deserve it, because that's when I really need it.» - Neil Gaiman

#756 «Love is a springtime plant that perfumes everything with its hope, even the ruins to which it clings.» - Gustave Flaubert

#757 «We picture love as heart-shaped because we do not know the shape of the soul.» - Robert Breault

#758 «He who is in love with himself has at least this advantage - he won't encounter many rivals.» - Georg C. Lichtenberg

#759 «Blessed is the influence of one true, loving human soul on another.» - George Eliot

#760 «The noblest spirit is most strongly attracted by the love of glory.» - James A. Baldwin

#761 «True love makes the thought of death frequent, easy, without terrors; it merely becomes the standard of comparison, the price one would pay for many things.» - Stendhal

#762 «You could have had anything else in the world, and you asked for me." She smiled up at him. Filthy as he was, covered in blood and dirt, he was the most beautiful thing she'd ever seen. "But I don't want anything else in the world.» - Cassandra Clare

#763 «You really shouldn't say 'I love you' unless you mean it. But if you mean it, you should say it a lot. People forget.» - Jessica Jung

#764 «LEAD, n. A heavy blue-gray metal much used in giving stability to light lovers - particularly to those who love not wisely but other men's wives.» - Ambrose Bierce

#765 «By the accident of fortune a man may rule the world for a time, but by virtue of love and kindness he may rule the world forever.» - Laozi

#766 «Love is like an hourglass, with the heart filling up as the brain empties.» - Jules Renard

#767 «When I say it's you I like, I'm talking about that part of you that knows that life is far more than anything you can ever see or hear or touch. That deep part of you that allows you to stand for those things without which humankind cannot survive. Love that conquers hate, peace that rises triumphant over war, and justice that proves more powerful than greed.» - Fred Rogers

#768 «Soul meets soul on lovers' lips.» - Percy Bysshe Shelley

#769 «Love is the perception of individuals. Love is the extremely difficult realisation that something other than oneself is real.» - Iris Murdoch

#770 «The music in his laughter had a way of rounding off the missing notes in her soul.» - Gloria Naylor

#771 «Life is the flower for which love is the honey.» - Victor Hugo

#772 «Your words are my food, your breath my wine. You are everything to me.» - Sarah Bernhardt

#773 «Ah me! why may not love and life be one?» - Henry Timrod

#774 «You don't walk away if you love someone. You help the person.» - Hillary Clinton

#775 «Peace cannot be kept by force; it can only be achieved by understanding.» - Albert Einstein

#776 «Laugh as much as you breathe and love as long as you live.» - Johnny Depp

#777 «Sure, love vincit omnia; is immeasurably above all ambition, more precious than wealth, more noble than name. He knows not life who knows not that: he hath not felt the highest faculty of the soul who hath not enjoyed it.» - William Makepeace Thackeray

#778 «The greatest thing you'll ever learn

Is just to love and be loved in return.» - Eden Ahbez"

#779 «deeds cannot dream what dreams can do» - e. e. cummings

#780 «Sometimes love means letting go when you want to hold on tighter.» - Melissa Marr

#781 «To love means to open ourselves to the negative as well as the positive - to grief, sorrow, and disappointment as well as to joy, fulfillment, and an intensity of consciousness we did not know was possible before» - Rollo May

#782 «Lost love is still love. It takes a different form, that's all. You can't see their smile or bring them food or tousle their hair or move them around a dance floor. But when those senses weaken another heightens. Memory. Memory becomes your partner. You nurture it. You hold it. You dance with it.» - Mitch Albom

#783 «Send the haters all my love. X and O.» - Drake

#784 «Love is a canvas furnished by Nature and embroidered by imagination.» - Voltaire

#785 «I opened myself to you only to be skinned alive. The more vulnerable I became, the faster and more deft your knife. Knowing what was happening, still I stayed and let you carve more. That's how much I loved you. That's how much.» - Rabih Alameddine

#786 «Love is the answer, and you know that for sure;
Love is a flower, you've got to let it grow.» - John Lennon"

#787 «You know it's love when all you want is that person
to be happy, even if you're not part of their happiness.» -
Julia Roberts

#788 «Gather therefore the Rose, whilst yet is prime, For
soon comes age, that will her pride deflower: Gather the
Rose of love, whilst yet is time.» - Edmund Spenser

#789 «The moment you have in your heart this
extraordinary thing called love and feel the depth, the
delight, the ecstasy of it, you will discover that for you the
world is transformed.» - Jiddu Krishnamurti

#790 «We understand death for the first time when he
puts his hand upon one whom we love» - Madame de Stael

#791 «Those who don't know how to weep with their
whole heart, don't know how to laugh either.» - Golda
Meir

#792 «Love is the beginning, the middle, and the end of
everything.» - Jean-Baptiste Henri Lacordaire

#793 «As far as the education of children is concerned I think they should be taught not the little virtues but the great ones. Not thrift but generosity and an indifference to money; not caution but courage and a contempt for danger; not shrewdness but frankness and a love of truth; not tact but love for one's neighbor and self-denial; not a desire for success but a desire to be and to know.» - Natalia Ginzburg

#794 «We like someone because. We love someone although.» - Henry de Montherlant

#795 «Do you love your creator Love your fellow-beings first.» - Muhammad

#796 «If you love someone, set them free. If they come back they're yours; if they don't they never were.» - Richard Bach

#797 «Take love when love is given.» - Sara Teasdale

#798 «A purpose of human life, no matter who is controlling it, is to love whoever is around to be loved.» - Kurt Vonnegut

#799 «He who loves not women, wine, and song Remains a fool his whole life long.» - Martin Luther

#800 «Sometimes the break in your heart is like the hole in the flute. Sometimes it's the place where the music comes through.» - Andrea Gibson

#801 «So, fall asleep love, loved by me... for I know love, I am loved by thee.» - Robert Browning

#802 «Miracles occur naturally as expressions of love. The real miracle is the love that inspires them. In this sense everything that comes from love is a miracle.» - Marianne Williamson

#803 «I want you any way I can get you. Not because you're beautiful or clever or kind or adorable, although devil knows you're all those things. I want you because there's no one else like you, and I don't ever want to start a day without seeing you.» - Lisa Kleypas

#804 «Love the animals, love the plants, love everything. If you love everything, you will perceive the divine mystery in things. Once you perceive it, you will begin to comprehend it better every day. And you will come at last to love the whole world with an all-embracing love.» - Fyodor Dostoevsky

#805 «Every poem is a momentary stay against the confusion of the world.» - Robert Frost

#806 «Wisdom delights in water; love delights in hills. Wisdom is stirring; love is quiet. Wisdom is merry; love grows old.» - Confucius

#807 «It is difficult to know at what moment love begins; it is less difficult to know that it has begun.» - Henry Wadsworth Longfellow

#808 «Love is anterior to life, posterior to death, initial of creation, and the exponent of breath.» - Emily Dickinson

#809 «The most important things to do in the world are to get something to eat, something to drink and somebody to love you.» - Brendan Behan

#810 «The most important thing in life is to learn how to give out love, and to let it come in.» - Morrie Schwartz

#811 «The fickleness of the women I love is only equalled by the infernal constancy of the women who love me.» - George Bernard Shaw

#812 «Someday you'll find someone special again. People who've been in love once usually do. It's in their nature.» - Nicholas Sparks

#813 «Love touched her heart, and lo! It beats high, and burns with such brave hearts.» - Richard Crawshaw

#814 «To love and be loved is to feel the sun from both sides.» - David Viscott

#815 «I believe that food is one way to make people happy. I also believe that food can unite people from all walks of life and cultures. When we sit together and eat, we promote better understanding and harmony.Food brings love, peace and compassion to the table.» - Chef Wan

#816 «A husband is what is left of a lover, after the nerve has been extracted.» - Helen Rowland

#817 «There is love of course. And then there's life, its enemy.» - Jean Anouilh

#818 «Haters are just confused admirers because they can't figure out the reason why everyone loves you.» - Jeffree Star

#819 «One day you will ask me which is more important? My life or yours? I will say mine and you will walk away not knowing that you are my life.» - Khalil Gibran

#820 «He who joyfully marches to music in rank and file has already earned my contempt. He has been given a large brain by mistake, since for him the spinal cord would suffice.» - Albert Einstein

#821 «We always come back to our first love.» - Etienne Aigner

#822 «Your mind was made to know and love God.» - John Piper

#823 «Let us not be satisfied with just giving money. Money is not enough, money can be got, but they need your hearts to love them. So, spread your love everywhere you go.» - Mother Teresa

#824 «Life, he realize, was much like a song. In the beginning there is mystery, in the end there is confirmation, but it's in the middle where all the emotion resides to make the whole thing worthwhile.» - Nicholas Sparks

#825 «A woman's heart should be so hidden in God that a man has to seek Him just to find her.» - Max Lucado

#826 «Let the wife make the husband glad to come home, and let him make her sorry to see him leave.» - Martin Luther

#827 «Be patient toward all that is unsolved in your heart.» - Rainer Maria Rilke

#828 «No, no the mind I love must still have wild places - a tangled orchard where dark damsons drop in the heavy grass, an overgrown litde wood, the chance of a snake or two (real snakes), a pool that nobody's fathomed the depth of, and paths threaded with those litde flowers planted by the wind.» - Katherine Mansfield

#829 «Somewhere the sense makes copper roses steel roses — The rose carried weight of love but love is at an end — of roses It is at the edge of the petal that love waits.» - William Carlos Williams

#830 «Cherish your visions. Cherish your ideals. Cherish the music that stirs in your heart, the beauty that forms in your mind, the loveliness that drapes your purest thoughts. For out of them will grow all delightful conditions, all heavenly environment, of these, if you but remain true to them, your world will at last be built.» - James Allen

#831 «Love sacrifices all things to bless the thing it loves.» - Edward Bulwer-Lytton, 1st Baron Lytton

#832 «If you say, I love you, then you have already fallen in love with language, which is already a form of break up and infidelity.» - Jean Baudrillard

#833 «I love you the more in that I believe you had liked me for my own sake and for nothing else.» - John Keats

#834 «Men always want to be a woman's first love - women like to be a man's last romance.» - Oscar Wilde

#835 «Only love can break your heart.» - Neil Young

#836 «That love is reverence, and worship, and glory, and the upward glance. Not a bandage for dirty sores. But they don't know it. Those who speak of love most promiscuously are the ones who've never felt it. They make some sort of feeble stew out of sympathy, compassion, contempt, and general indifference, and they call it love. Once you've felt what it means to love as you and I know it – the total passion for the total height – you're incapable of anything less.» - Ayn Rand

#837 «My only love sprung from my only hate.» - William Shakespeare

#838 «The foundation stones for a balanced success are honesty, character, integrity, faith, love and loyalty.» - Zig Ziglar

#839 «Sometimes the heart sees what is invisible to the eye.» - H. Jackson Brown, Jr.

#840 «Let me not to the marriage of true minds» - William Shakespeare

#841 «I believe that imagination is stronger than knowledge. That myth is more potent than history. That dreams are more powerful than facts. That hope always triumphs over experience. That laughter is the only cure for grief. And I believe that love is stronger than death.» - Robert Fulghum

#842 «We can't form our children on our own concepts; we must take them and love them as God gives them to us.» - Johann Wolfgang von Goethe

#843 «Love is metaphysical gravity.» - R. Buckminster Fuller

#844 «Gamble everything for love, if you're a true human being.» - Rumi

#845 «Only love expands intelligence. To live in love is to accept the other and the conditions of his existence as a source of richness, not as opposition, restriction or limitation.» - Humberto Maturana

#846 «Let the sun stop burning,
Let them tell me love's not worth going through.
If it all falls apart,
I will know deep in my heart,
The only dream that mattered had come true

...In this life I was loved by you.» - Bette Midler"

#847 «A DEFINITION NOT FOUND IN THE DICTIONARY Not leaving: an act of trust and love, often deciphered by children» - Markus Zusak

#848 «Harmony is pure love, for love is a concerto.» - Lope de Vega

#849 «It is a rare and beautiful thing when we choose to offer love in situations when most people would choose to scorn or ignore.» - Lysa TerKeurst

#850 «We don't believe in rheumatism and true love until after the first attack.» - Marie von Ebner-Eschenbach

#851 «And I'd choose you; in a hundred lifetimes, in a hundred worlds, in any version of reality, I'd find you and I'd choose you.» - Kiersten White

#852 «When you give each other everything, it becomes an even trade. Each wins all.» - Lois McMaster Bujold

#853 «It is by loving and not by being loved that one can come nearest to the soul of another.» - George MacDonald

#854 «Beauty kindles love, and only the one who remains captivated by it, only the one who is intoxicated by it, only the one who remains a lover while he is investigating its essence, can hope to penetrate its essence.» - Dietrich von Hildebrand

#855 «Love, and you shall be loved.» - Ralph Waldo Emerson

#856 «I have a history of making decisions very quickly about men. I have always fallen in love fast and without measuring risks. I have a tendency not only to see the best in everyone, but to assume that everyone is emotionally capable of reaching his highest potential. I have fallen in love more times than I care to count with the highest potential of a man, rather than with the man himself, and I have hung on to the relationship for a long time (sometimes far too long) waiting for the man to ascend to his own greatness. Many times in romance I have been a victim of my own optimism.» - Elizabeth Gilbert

#857 «I try to give to the poor people for love what the rich could get for money. No, I wouldn't touch a leper for a thousand pounds; yet I willingly cure him for the love of God.» - Mother Teresa

#858 «to love is to risk, not being loved in return. to hope is to risk pain. to try is to risk failure. but risk must be taken because the greatest hazard in my life is to risk nothing.» - Bob Marley

#859 «They do not love that do not show their love. The course of true love never did run smooth. Love is a familiar. Love is a devil. There is no evil angel but Love.» - William Shakespeare

#860 «Love is what we were born with. Fear is what we learned here.» - Marianne Williamson

#861 «True love stories never have endings.» - Richard Bach

#862 «One of the hardest things in life is having words in your heart that you can't utter.» - James Earl Jones

#863 «Who, being loved, is poor?» - Oscar Wilde

#864 «Something we were withholding made us weak, until we found it was ourselves.» - Robert Frost

#865 «Absence from those we love is self from self - a deadly banishment.» - William Shakespeare

#866 «Love is my religion - I could die for it.» - John Keats

#867 «And then, strange to say, the first symptom of true love in a young man is timidity; in a girl, it is boldness.» - Victor Hugo

#868 «I have feelings too. I am still human. All I want is to be loved, for myself and for my talent.» - Marilyn Monroe

#869 «Knowing how to be solitary is central to the art of loving. When we can be alone, we can be with others without using them as a means of escape.» - Bell Hooks

#870 «The love of life is necessary to the vigorous prosecution of any undertaking» - Samuel Johnson

#871 «Give me love Give me love Give me peace on earth Give me light Give me life Keep me free from birth Give me hope Help me cope, with this heavy load Trying to, touch and reach you with, heart and soul» - George Harrison

#872 «To be able to say how much love, is love but little.» - Petrarch

#873 «Love is the beauty of the soul.» - Saint Augustine

#874 «All mankind love a lover.» - Ralph Waldo Emerson

#875 «You cannot help another who will not help him or herself. In the end, all souls must walk their path - and the reason they are walking a particular path may not be clear to us... or even to them at the level of ordinary human consciousness. Do what you can to help others, of course. Show love and caring whenever and wherever you can. But do not get caught up in someone else's "story" to the point where you start writing it.» - Neale Donald Walsch

#876 «There's a crack (or cracks) in everyone...that's how the light of God gets in.» - Elizabeth Gilbert

#877 «Love costs all we are
and will ever be.
Yet it is only love
which sets us free.

A Brave and Startling Truth.» - Maya Angelou"

#878 «I Cannot Exist Without You. I Am Forgetful Of Everything But Seeing You Again.» - John Keats

#879 «There is hardly a more gracious gift that we can offer somebody than to accept them fully, to love them almost despite themselves.» - Elizabeth Gilbert

#880 «In a universe of ambiguity, this kind of certainty comes only once, and never again, no matter how many lifetimes you live.» - Robert James Waller

#881 «The thought manifests as the word. The word manifests as the deed. The deed develops into habit. And the habit hardens into character. So watch the thought and its ways with care. And let it spring from love, born out of concern for all beings.» - Gautama Buddha

#882 «Love is the crowning grace of humanity, the holiest right of the soul, the golden link which binds us to duty and truth, the redeeming principle that chiefly reconciles the heart to life, and is prophetic of eternal good.» - Petrarch

#883 «Marriage is a great institution, but I'm not ready for an institution.» - Mae West

#884 «And now here is my secret, a very simple secret; it is only with the heart that one can see rightly, what is essential is invisible to the eye.» - Antoine de Saint-Exupery

#885 «There is nothing--no circumstance, no trouble, no testing--that can ever touch me until, first of all, it has gone past God and past Christ right through to me. If it has come that far, it has come with a great purpose, which I may not understand at the moment. But as I refuse to become panicky, as I lift up my eyes to Him and accept it as coming from the throne of God for some great purpose of blessing to my own heart, no sorrow will ever disturb me, no circumstance will cause me to fret, for I shall rest in the joy of what my Lord is--that is the rest of victory!» - Alan Redpath

#886 «The awakening is the purpose. The awakening of the fact that in essence we are light, we are love. Each cell of our body, each cell and molecule of everything. The power source that runs all life is light. So to awaken to that knowledge, and to desire to operate in that realm, and to believe that it is possible, are all factors that will put you there.» - Dolores Cannon

#887 «Let men tremble to win the hand of woman, unless they win along with it the utmost passion of her heart!» - Nathaniel Hawthorne

#888 «It is an extra dividend when you like the girl you've fallen in love with.» - Clark Gable

#889 «A half-read book is a half-finished love affair.» - David Mitchell

#890 «Love is composed of a single soul inhabiting two bodies.» - Aristotle

#891 «Whether life is worth living depends on whether there is love in life.» - R. D. Laing

#892 «When you trip over love, it is easy to get up. But when you fall in love, it is impossible to stand again.» - Albert Einstein

#893 «A dog is the only thing on earth that loves you more than you love yourself.» - Josh Billings

#894 «It is sad not to love, but it is much sadder not to be able to love.» - Miguel de Unamuno

#895 «Love is not in our choice but in our fate.» - John Dryden

#896 «When someone is in your heart, they're never truly gone. They can come back to you, even at unlikely times.» - Mitch Albom

#897 «But love is much like a dam; if you allow a tiny crack to form through which only a trickle of water can pass, that trickle will quickly bring down the whole structure and soon no one will be able to control the force of the current.» - Paulo Coelho

#898 «Love alone is capable of uniting living beings in such a way as to complete and fulfill them, for it alone takes them and joins them by what is deepest in themselves.» - Pierre Teilhard de Chardin

#899 «In ancient China, the Taoists taught that a constant inner smile, a smile to oneself, insured health, happiness and longevity. Why? Smiling to yourself is like basking in love: you become your own best friend. Living with an inner smile is to live in harmony with yourself.» - Mantak Chia

#900 «Love is the symbol of eternity.» - Madame de Stael

#901 «Just because you're beautiful and perfect, it's made you conceited.» - William Goldman

#902 «When we first met, I didn't want to get involved with anyone. I didn't have the time or energy, and I wasn't sure that I was ready for it. But you were so good to me, and I got swept up in that. And little by little, I found myself falling in love with you.» - Nicholas Sparks

#903 «Towards the outside, at any rate, the ego seems to maintain clear and sharp lines of demarcation. There is only one state -- admittedly an unusual state, but not one that can be stigmatized as pathological -- in which it does not do this. At the height of being in love the boundary between ego and object threatens to melt away. Against all the evidence of his senses, a man who is in love declares that "I" and "you" are one, and is prepared to behave as if it were a fact.» - Sigmund Freud

#904 «Love means to commit oneself without guarantee, to give oneself completely in the hope that our love will produce love in the loved person. Love is an act of faith, and whoever is of little faith is also of little love.» - Erich Fromm

#905 «When I pray for another person, I am praying for God to open my eyes so that I can see that person as God does, and then enter into the stream of love that God already directs toward that person.» - Philip Yancey

#906 «Half the world is composed of people who have something to say and can't, and the other half who have nothing to say and keep on saying it.» - Robert Frost

#907 «To find someone who will love you for no reason, and to shower that person with reasons, that is the ultimate happiness.» - Robert Breault

#908 «That man is a success who has lived well, laughed often and loved much.» - Robert Louis Stevenson

#909 «Oh my luve's like a red, red rose,
That's newly sprung in June;
Oh my luve's like the melodie
That's sweetly played in tune.» - Robert Burns"

#910 «Love is eternal, the aspect may change, but not the essence.» - Vincent Van Gogh

#911 «Love seeks no cause beyond itself and no fruit; it is its own fruit, its own enjoyment. I love because I love; I love in order that I may love.» - Bernard of Clairvaux

#912 «The devotion of thought to an honest achievement makes the achievement possible. Exceptions only confirm this rule, proving that failure is occasioned by a too feeble faith.» - Mary Baker Eddy

#913 «Love is a state in which a man sees things most decidedly as they are not.» - Friedrich Nietzsche

#914 «Love must be as much a light as it is a flame.» - Henry David Thoreau

#915 «For what is love itself, for the one we love best? An enfolding of immeasurable cares which yet are better than any joys outside our love.» - George Eliot

#916 «The world was collapsing, and the only thing that really mattered to me was that she was alive.» - Rick Riordan

#917 «In love, one and one are one.» - Jean-Paul Sartre

#918 «It is not true that love makes all things easy; it makes us choose what is difficult.» - George Eliot

#919 «You will soon break the bow if you keep it always stretched.» - Norman Vincent Peale

#920 «The fate of love is that it always seems too little or too much.» - Amelia Barr

#921 «Our God is abundant in love and steadfast in mercy. He saves us, not because we trust in a symbol, but because we trust in a Savior.» - Max Lucado

#922 «He prayeth best, who loveth best All things both great and small; For the dear God who loveth us, He made and loveth all.» - Samuel Taylor Coleridge

#923 «A thing of beauty is a joy for ever: Its loveliness increases; it will never Pass into nothingness; but still will keep A bower quiet for us, and a sleep Full of sweet dreams, and health, and quiet breathing.» - John Keats

#924 «To love another person you have to undertake some fragment of their destiny.» - Quentin Crisp

#925 «The distinction between the past, present and future is only a stubbornly persistent illusion.» - Albert Einstein

#926 «Life is too short to be anything but real with the cast of characters God has placed in the story of your life. Love well, laugh often, and find your life in Christ. Don't hide away or be a follower. Be the wonderful unique person God made you to be, and know that your purpose will always be best when defined by your faith in him» - Karen Kingsbury

#927 «To live in this world, you must be able to do three things: to love what is mortal; to hold it against your bones knowing your own life depends on it; and, when the time comes to let it go, to let it go.» - Mary Oliver

#928 «Love is a great beautifier.» - Louisa May Alcott

#929 «Love as much as you can from wherever you are.» - Thaddeus Golas

#930 «He bent his head and kissed her long and deeply, and in that kiss neither knew themselves, or even each other, but something beyond all consciousness that was both of them.» - Eleanor Farjeon

#931 «Hate leaves ugly scars, love leaves beautiful ones.» - Mignon McLaughlin

#932 «Give me the end of the year an' its fun

When most of the plannin' an' toilin' is done;
Bring all the wanderers home to the nest,

Let me sit down with the ones I love best,
Hear the old voices still ringin' with song,

See the old faces unblemished by wrong,
See the old table with all of its chairs

An' I'll put soul in my Thanksgivin' prayers.» - Edgar Guest"

#933 «You know my God. My God is called love» - Mother Teresa

#934 «Love is no assignment for cowards.» - Ovid

#935 «Things didn't work between the two of them, because they loved the same person. He loved her and she loved herself» - Ravinder Singh

#936 «Once the realization is accepted that even between the closest human beings infinite distances continue, a wonderful living side by side can grow, if they succeed in loving the distance between them which makes it possible for each to see the other whole against the sky.» - Rainer Maria Rilke

#937 «The things that we love tell us what we are.» - Thomas Aquinas

#938 «We are born to love, we live to love, and we will die to love still more.» - Saint Joseph

#939 «For you see, each day I love you more. Today more than yesterday and less than tomorrow.» - Rosemonde Gerard

#940 «Come live in my heart, and pay no rent.» - Samuel Lover

#941 «Down on your knees, and thank heaven, fasting, for a good man's love.» - Euripides

#942 «Love and doubt have never been on speaking terms.» - Khalil Gibran

#943 «If we lose love and self respect for each other, this is how we finally die.» - Maya Angelou

#944 «The greatest happiness of life is the conviction that we are loved; loved for ourselves, or rather, loved in spite of ourselves.» - Victor Hugo

#945 «Love shall be our token; love be yours and love be mine.» - Christina Rossetti

#946 «Love is an act of endless forgiveness, a tender look which becomes a habit.» - Peter Ustinov

#947 «As soon as beauty is sought not from religion and love, but for pleasure, it degrades the seeker.» - Annie Dillard

#948 «O, my luve is like a red, red rose.» - Robert Burns

#949 «Just as we take for granted the need to acquire proficiency in the basic academic subjects, I am hopeful that a time will come when we can take it for granted that children will learn, as part of the curriculum, the indispensability of inner values: love, compassion, justice, and forgiveness.» - Dalai Lama

#950 «True love is usually the most inconvenient kind.» - Kiera Cass

#951 «To love and win is the best thing. To love and lose, the next best.» - William Makepeace Thackeray

#952 «To love for the sake of being loved is human, but to love for the sake of loving is angelic.» - Alphonse de Lamartine

#953 «A pity beyond all telling is hid in the heart of love.» - William Butler Yeats

#954 «The sweetest joy, the wildest woe is love.» - Pearl Bailey

#955 «May you live as long as you wish and love as long as you live.» - Robert A. Heinlein

#956 «I heard what you said. I'm not the silly romantic you think. I don't want the heavens or the shooting stars. I don't want gemstones or gold. I have those things already. I want...a steady hand. A kind soul. I want to fall asleep, and wake, knowing my heart is safe. I want to love, and be loved.» - Shana Abe

#957 «Alcohol may be man's worst enemy, but the bible says love your enemy.» - Frank Sinatra

#958 «O, thou art fairer than the evening air clad in the beauty of a thousand stars.» - Christopher Marlowe

#959 «Men have died from time to time, and worms have eaten them, but not for love.» - William Shakespeare

#960 «People who are not in love fail to understand how an intelligent man can suffer because of a very ordinary woman. This is like being surprised that anyone should be stricken with cholera because of a creature so insignificant as the common bacillus.» - Marcel Proust

#961 «Grow old with me! The best is yet to be.» - Robert Browning

#962 «Love brings to life whatever is dead around us.» - Franz Rosenzweig

#963 «Keep love in your heart. A life without it is like a sunless garden when the flowers are dead. The consciousness of loving and being loved brings a warmth and a richness to life that nothing else can bring.» - Oscar Wilde

#964 «Love involves a peculiar unfathomable combination of understanding and misunderstanding.» - Diane Arbus

#965 «If you love something let it go free. If it doesn't come back, you never had it. If it comes back, love it forever.» - Douglas Horton

#966 «Pursue some path, however narrow and crooked, in which you can walk with love and reverence.» - Henry David Thoreau

#967 «I love that feeling of being in love, the effect of having butterflies when you wake up in the morning. That is special.» - Jennifer Aniston

#968 «The first duty of love is to listen.» - Paul Tillich

#969 «There is the same difference in a person before and after he is in love, as there is in an unlighted lamp and one that is burning.» - Vincent Van Gogh

#970 «Some women love only what they can hold in their arms; others, only what they can't.» - Mignon McLaughlin

#971 «Love hard when there is love to be had. Because perfect guys don't exist, but there's always one guy that is perfect for you.» - Bob Marley

#972 «I think I fell in love with her, a little bit. Isn't that dumb? But it was like I knew her. Like she was my oldest, dearest friend. The kind of person you can tell anything to, no matter how bad, and they'll still love you, because they know you. I wanted to go with her. I wanted her to notice me. And then she stopped walking. Under the moon, she stopped. And looked at us. She looked at me. Maybe she was trying to tell me something; I don't know. She probably didn't even know I was there. But I'll always love her. All my life.» - Neil Gaiman

#973 «Sometimes people put up walls, not to keep others out, but to see who cares enough to break them down.» - Banana Yoshimoto

#974 «I was born when you kissed me. I died when you left me. I lived a few weeks while you loved me.» - Humphrey Bogart

#975 «I've only been in love with a beer bottle and a mirror.» - Sid Vicious

#976 «Like the measles, love is most dangerous when it comes late in life.» - Lord Byron

#977 «Love is the big booming beat which covers up the noise of hate.» - Margaret Cho

#978 «As her father had so often said... Laugh as much as you breathe and love as long as you live.» - Sherrilyn Kenyon

#979 «Some Cupid kills with arrows, some with traps.» - William Shakespeare

#980 «You can't blame gravity for falling in love.» - Albert Einstein

#981 «You know what I am going to say. I love you. What other men may mean when they use that expression, I cannot tell; what I mean is, that I am under the influence of some tremendous attraction which I have resisted in vain, and which overmasters me.» - Charles Dickens

#982 «If it is your time, love will track you down like a cruise missile.» - Lynda Barry

#983 «Jesus said love one another. He didn't say love the whole world.» - Mother Teresa

#984 «Girls we love for what they are; young men for what they promise to be.» - Johann Wolfgang von Goethe

#985 «Truth is everybody is going to hurt you: you just gotta find the ones worth suffering for.» - Bob Marley

#986 «To Almighty God, it's not how much we give, but how much love we put in the giving. Love is not measured by how much we do; love is measured by how much love we put in; how much it is hurting us in loving.» - Mother Teresa

#987 «It isn't possible to love and part. You will wish that it was. You can transmute love, ignore it, muddle it, but you can never pull it out of you. I know by experience that the poets are right: love is eternal.» - E. M. Forster

#988 «There is no limit to the power of loving.» - John Morton

Made in United States
North Haven, CT
26 June 2023

38237723R00087